"Galilee By The Sea"
by Claudy Barnes

Loaves & Fishes

5TH EDITION

A COOKBOOK FROM GALILEE CHURCH
VIRGINIA BEACH, VIRGINIA

Cover painting: *Fish,* Betty Herbert

Paintings: *Galilee by the Sea,* Claudy Barnes; *St. Luke's Chapel,* Jane Sautter; *Fun in the Garden,* Margolith Doron; *Workers in the Field,* David Freyss; *The Chef,* Sara Moore; *Spanish Fisherman,* Carol DeBolt Eikenberry; *Beets,* Helen Z. Chilton; *Summer Bounty,* Libby Bennett; *Avignon Alfresco,* William Campbell

ISBN 0-9759286-0-0

WIMMER
COOKBOOKS

A CONSOLIDATED GRAPHICS COMPANY

800.548.2537   wimmerco.com

$\mathcal{T}$ABLE OF $\mathcal{C}$ONTENTS

A Message from Our Rector

Dear Friends,

Jesus enjoyed good food, and loved sharing it with good friends. Many times in our Lord's earthly ministry we find Him dining with friends. Several instances come to mind....

- When He attended the wedding reception—John 2.

- When He attended Matthew, the Tax Collector's, dinner party—Luke 5.

- When He fed 5000 men (many more with women and children!) bread and fish—Matthew 14.

- When He ate fish with His disciples after the resurrection—John 21.

- When He shared the Last Supper gathering with His disciples— Matthew 26.

The Scriptures remind us that God is the source of all good gifts, and gives them to us richly to enjoy. That includes good food and good friends!

May the wonderful recipes we find in these pages promote hospitality, love, and welcome in our homes and hearts. (These recipes will undoubtedly be so delicious that we'll have to remember "moderation in all things!")

So as you gather around the tables of family and friends, may you "taste and see that the Lord is good." And in dining together and sharing fellowship, may we all remember the One in our midst, and give Him thanks and praise for His goodness.

What a great invitation from the risen Christ to His first disciples, and to us today.... "Come, and dine!...." (John 21:12).

God's blessings to you and your family,

Coleman Tyler
Rector

PS: A warm and grateful "thank-you" to all who have worked so faithfully on this project: Suzanne Ganschinietz, Marian Kitchin, Lorna St. George, Dale Wilson and all their very capable volunteers. Thanks!

*I*NTRODUCTION

We are very fortunate in this church; very few of us have been in the presence of, or experienced, starvation—the need for food when none is available, and no hope of any. Food and feeding are commonplace for us. Churches produce cookbooks to remind us of our luxury in this area of our lives and to remind us of how God's Grace is shown through the life and sacrifice of His Son Jesus. We trust as you use these recipes from the Christians in Galilee Church you will be reminded of God's gracious feeding through the Power and Presence of His Holy Spirit!

For the bread of God is He which comes down from heaven and gives life to the world.

—John 6:33

John H. Jordan, Jr.

John H. Jordan, Rector *Emeritus*

${\mathcal{A}}$CKNOWLEDGEMENTS

This edition of *Loaves & Fishes* is the fifth in a series of cookbooks published by the Women of Galilee. It celebrates over 100 years of Galilee Church as well as all of the excellent cooks in our parish. We are pleased to be able to include recipes that have stood the test of time as well as some special recipes from well known restaurants in and around the Tidewater area. The Women of Galilee are grateful for every recipe contributed and for the hard work of so many to make this *Loaves & Fishes* a special book.

A special debt of gratitude is owed to the artists at The Artists' Gallery, Virginia Beach, Virginia. These local artists have contributed many hours to the design of this book. All of the paintings that appear on the color pages are original works by several of these local artists. Betty Herbert has kindly donated her painting, *Fish,* to Galilee Church.

"Saint Luke's Chapel"
by Jane Sautter

Church History

$\mathcal{A}$ $\mathcal{B}$RIEF $\mathcal{H}$ISTORY OF $\mathcal{G}$ALILEE $\mathcal{C}$HURCH, *1895-2004*

The history of Galilee Church closely parallels the development of Virginia Beach as a resort city. Galilee grew from a small mission church to one of the largest congregations in the Diocese of Southern Virginia as Virginia Beach grew from a small rural coastal town to a flourishing resort city.

Many Norfolk residents were attracted to the sleepy resort and spent their vacations enjoying the beach. Among them was the Reverend Beverly D. Tucker, the rector of Old St. Paul's Church and later Bishop of the Diocese. Tucker Cottage, his residence, was located on the oceanfront at 18th Street. In the late 1880s, the Tuckers invited neighbors to gather at their cottage for Sunday morning worship.

In the 1880s and 1890s, there was no church in Virginia Beach for worship by any congregation. Frustrated by the lack of a place of worship, three prominent Norfolk businessmen met one Sunday afternoon on the verandah of the Princess Anne Hotel. They decided to raise funds for an interdenominational chapel at the resort. Enough money was raised to purchase a lot on the oceanfront at 18th Street. A small frame church was built and was called Union Chapel. The Chapel was ecumenical. Each Sunday began with a Catholic Mass, followed by the Presbyterian and Episcopal services with the Baptists and the Methodists worshipping in the afternoon and evening.

By 1895, Union Chapel was leased to Eastern Shore Chapel at the same time that an Episcopal Mission was established at Virginia Beach. The rector of the Eastern Shore Chapel, the Reverend William S. Savage, served the new mission and gave it the name "Galilee by the Sea."

The Reverend Savage often spent winters at Tucker Cottage. He not only preached but also played the organ and directed the choirs. He had a small portable organ that he carried with him. This small organ, crafted around 1885, found its way back to Galilee in the spring of 2003. It was played for the congregation by Galilee's present rector, the musically gifted Rev. Dr. Coleman Tyler. In his sermon that day he described the joy of playing and pumping the little organ, achieving a fairly good aerobic workout in the process. This organ is now located in St. Luke's Chapel.

Galilee by the Sea ceased to be a mission in 1903. By the 1920s, beach erosion and a growing congregation necessitated that a new church be built. The new brick church building on 18th Street was completed in 1926 and was dedicated to the honor of Bishop Tucker. The original frame church was moved behind this new structure and was named Tucker Hall. It served as the parish house for many years. The church faced the ocean and many of Galilee's older parishioners remember the smells and sounds of the sea drifting in during the sermons.

World War II again brought change and an increase in population to the resort city. Tucker Hall served as a club run by Galilee for enlisted men. When the need for a larger parish house arose, a new rectory was purchased on 53rd Street. During the 1940s, both Eastern Shore and Galilee grew in membership and could no longer be served by one rector. The vestries decided that each church should function separately. Galilee's congregation received parish status within the diocese.

By the 1950s, continued growth required that a new church be built to meet the needs of the congregation. Ground-breaking for the third and present structure took place in July of 1956.

Membership and ministries have continued to grow at Galilee and renovations and expansions have been necessary to accommodate this growth. A new wing was built in the late 1980s. St. Luke's Chapel, St. Andrew's Chapel and Tucker Hall are located in this wing. The small St. Luke's Chapel is the healing chapel. The Scripture *"Come unto me all ye who are weary and heavy laden"* is sewn on the red needlepoint kneeling cushions. Beautiful stained glass and church furniture from the original Galilee by the Sea are located in here as well.

More lovely needlepoint cushions and kneelers with designs of sea creatures are found in St. Andrew's Chapel. This needlework, like that in St. Luke's Chapel, was done by a small group of Galilee women. In the 1970s, several women in the congregation suggested that money be donated for kneelers in memory of parishioners who had died. A small needlework group was formed. These ladies originally commissioned a woman at the National Cathedral to design kneelers for Galilee. When her designs were found disappointing, parishioner Chamie Grandy created her own designs for the cushions. These were so lovely that soon she and another member of the

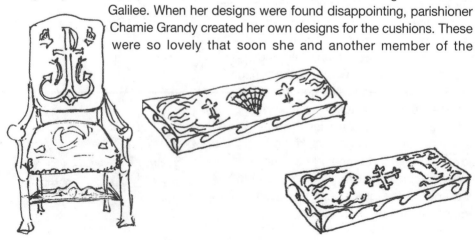

congregation, Ginny Bell, were traveling up and down the East coast designing needlepoint accessories for over sixty churches. They also designed the acolyte, ministerial, and chair cushions for Galilee's sanctuary.

In 1999 another expansion of the church was begun. This addition includes the large Celebration Center and has nearly doubled the church's physical space. In April 2002 the first service, a contemporary service, was held in the new Celebration Center. This weekly contemporary service continued in the Celebration Center until July, 2004. It was moved back into the sanctuary because the Celebration Center could no longer accommodate the number of people regularly in attendance. In May of 2002, the Bishop of the Diocese of Southern Virginia, the Right Reverend David Bane, dedicated the new addition to the Glory of God.

After Galilee ceased to be a mission in 1903, the first rector was the Reverend Edward Patton Miner. He labored for twenty years to create a strong community church. He was succeeded by the Reverend John R. Millbank, an Anglican clergyman, who led the congregation for two years. The next rector was the Reverend Thomas L. Rideout, who served the church from 1925 to 1929. In 1930, the Reverend Reginald Eastman came and stayed for ten years. During the war years, from 1941 to 1954, the Reverend Stiles B. Lines served the church. In 1945, the Reverend Charles W. Carnan Jr., a retired chaplain, came and served as rector until 1948. The Reverend Edmund Berkeley followed the ministry of Reverend Carnan in 1949 and left Galilee in 1966 after a fruitful ministry.

The Reverend John H. Jordan Jr., one of the most beloved members of the Galilee family, was called by the vestry in 1967. He served as rector for twenty-three years, until 1992, and continues to serve as Rector *Emeritus.* During his tenure as rector many of Galilee's present ministries were created or expanded. He was a driving force behind establishing the Virginia Beach Free Clinic and he helped found the Sugar Plum Bakery. Years before public schools had special education classes, John Jordan was instrumental in providing educational programs for children with special needs. He also helped establish the existing Montessori school, the Children's House of Galilee.

The Reverend John D. Burley succeeded Mr. Jordan and served Galilee from 1993 to 2002. The Reverend Dr. Coleman Tyler was named Galilee's tenth rector in January, 2003.

God has richly blessed Galilee Church over the more than one hundred years of her history. Today our vision remains strong and heartfelt: to be a Christ-centered community that builds bridges of faith, hope and love to a world in need.

As we seek to love God and one another, we proclaim the Lord Jesus Christ through the power of the Holy Spirit in worship, ministry, healing and service.

We would like to acknowledge research on the history of Galilee provided by Louisa Venable Kyle in *The History of Eastern Shore Chapel and Lynnhaven Parish, 1642-1969.*

Recipe for Joy

Surrendering our lives:

> *"You will show me the path of life;*
> *In Your presence is fullness of joy;*
> *At Your right hand are pleasures Forevermore."*
>
> Psalm 16:11

Surrendering our minds:

> *"But for You who fear my name,*
> *The Sun of Righteousness will rise*
> *With healing in his Wings.*
> *And you will go free, leaping with joy*
> *Like calves let out to pasture."*
>
> Malachi 4:2

Surrendering our hearts:

> *"The Lord your God is in your midst.*
> *A victorious warrior.*
> *He will exult over you with joy*
> *He will quiet you in his love*
> *He will rejoice over you with shouts of joy."*
>
> Zephaniah 3:17

Surrendering our will:

> *"So shall My word be which goes*
> *Forth from My mouth;*
> *It shall not return to me empty.*
> *Without accomplishing what I desire,*
> *And without succeeding in the*
> *Matter for which I sent it.*
> *For you will go out with joy,*
> *And be led forth with peace;*
> *The mountains and the hills will*
> *Break forth into shouts of joy before you,*
> *And all the trees of the field will*
> *Clap their hands."*
>
> Isaiah 55:11-12

Susan Tyler

Susan Tyler

"Fun In The Garden"
by Margolith Doron

Appetizers & Beverages

Appetizers & Beverages

Curry Dip for Vegetables or Fruit

Yield: 1½ cups

1	cup mayonnaise	¼	teaspoon onion juice
6	tablespoons sour cream	1½	teaspoons seasoned salt
1	tablespoon curry powder	1	teaspoon lemon juice

- Combine mayonnaise, sour cream, curry powder, onion juice, seasoned salt and lemon juice.
- Refrigerate overnight to blend flavors.

Good with raw vegetables or fruit.

Fried Okra

Yield: 2 dozen

1	pound fresh okra	½	cup cracker meal
½	cup all-purpose flour		Salt to taste
½	cup milk		Shortening

- Wash okra and cut crosswise into ¼-inch slices. Season to taste with salt.
- Roll okra pieces in flour, then dip in milk. Roll in cracker meal.
- Melt enough shortening in a skillet to cover the okra slices. Fry until golden brown. Drain on paper towels.

Marinated Mushrooms

Yield: 4 cups

1	cup vinegar	4	teaspoons mustard seeds
1	cup oil	2	teaspoons onion salt
4	teaspoons dried basil	2	pounds fresh mushrooms or
4	teaspoons marjoram		2 (16-ounce) cans whole mushrooms

- Combine vinegar, oil, basil, marjoram, mustard seeds and onion salt.
- Place mushrooms in marinade overnight.

Artichoke Tapenade

Cheryl Jordan created this delicious recipe after touring in northern California where assorted tapenades are served with bread.

Yield: 1½ cups

1	(14-ounce) can artichoke hearts	1	large clove garlic
½	cup olive oil		Zest of 1 lemon
¼	cup walnuts or pine nuts	¼	cup mayonnaise
1½	tablespoons lemon juice	½	teaspoon salt
1	small, mild onion	½	teaspoon pepper
1	teaspoon dried chives	½	teaspoon dried basil
¼	teaspoon cayenne pepper	2	tablespoons fresh parsley, chopped
1	tablespoon capers		

■ Combine artichoke hearts, olive oil, nuts, lemon juice, onion, chives, cayenne pepper, capers, garlic, lemon zest, mayonnaise, salt, pepper, basil and parsley in a food processor. Pulse until coarsely chopped.

■ Chill. Serve with toasted French bread slices.

Vidalia Onion Spread

Yield: 2½ cups

½	cup white vinegar	4	Vidalia onions, very thinly sliced
2	cups sugar	½	cup mayonnaise
2	cups water	1	tablespoon celery seed

■ Mix the vinegar, sugar and water. Marinate the onion slices in the liquid for 4 hours. Drain and chop the onions very finely.

■ Blend mayonnaise and celery seed. Add chopped onions.

■ Serve with crackers.

CALIFORNIA DIP

Yield: 8 cups or 50 servings

1½ cups shredded and diced Swiss
    cheese
1½ cups shredded and diced Monterey
    Jack cheese
4   tomatoes, chopped
2   bunches green onion, chopped

2   (6-ounce) cans chopped black olives
2   (4-ounce) cans green chili peppers
1   (15.5-ounce) can black beans, rinsed
    and drained
3-4 drops hot pepper sauce
1   (8-ounce) bottle Italian dressing

■ Combine the Swiss cheese, Monterey Jack cheese, tomatoes, green onions, black olives, green chili peppers and black beans.

■ Stir in hot pepper sauce and Italian dressing and mix well.

This dish is delicious served with Tortilla chips and will keep in the refrigerator up to 3 weeks.

TOMATO-BASIL BRUSCHETTA

Yield: 12-16 servings

3   tablespoons olive oil
1   teaspoon balsamic vinegar
Salt and pepper to taste
8-12 ounces fresh mozzarella cheese,
    cubed

4-5 ripe tomatoes, wedged or 24 cherry
    tomatoes, halved
1   cup fresh basil leaves, chopped
1   loaf French or Italian bread, sliced
2-3 cloves garlic, peeled and halved

■ Preheat broiler.

■ Combine the olive oil, balsamic vinegar, salt and pepper and mix thoroughly. Add cheese, tomatoes and chopped basil. Fold until coated.

■ Place the bread slices on a baking sheet and broil until crisp and lightly browned on both sides. Rub the garlic pieces over each slice of bread and sprinkle a small amount of olive oil on each piece.

■ Spoon the tomato, basil and cheese mixture onto each bread slice and serve.

Roasted red peppers may be used instead of tomatoes.

Insalata Caprese

Yield: 6 servings

8	tomatoes, sliced	¼ cup extra-virgin olive oil
1	pound fresh mozzarella cheese	Salt (sea salt preferred)
½	cup fresh basil	Freshly ground black pepper

■ Alternate slices of mozzarella cheese and tomatoes on a platter. Garnish with fresh basil leaves.

■ Drizzle olive oil over all. Sprinkle with salt and pepper.

Cheese Biscuits

Yield: 4 to 5 dozen

1 stick butter, softened
1 (12-16 ounce) package shredded sharp Cheddar cheese
¼ teaspoon salt

1¼ cups flour
¼ teaspoon cayenne pepper
4 drops hot pepper sauce
Pecan halves

■ Blend butter and cheese. Fold in salt, flour, pepper and hot pepper sauce. Form dough into 3 rolls, each 1-inch in diameter. Chill for 24 hours.

■ Preheat oven to 350 degrees. Spray baking sheets with non-stick vegetable spray.

■ Slice dough into thin rounds and place on prepared baking sheet. Press a pecan half into top of each biscuit.

■ Bake 15 to 20 minutes. Cool and store in tin.

Cheese Ball

Yield: 1 cheese ball

½	pound bleu or Roquefort cheese	1	small onion, finely chopped
½	pound Cheddar cheese, grated		Salt and pepper to taste
1	(8-ounce) package cream cheese, softened		Chopped nuts

- Mix bleu and Cheddar cheeses. Add softened cream cheese, onion, salt and pepper.

- Roll into a ball. Roll the ball in the chopped nuts. Refrigerate until firm.

Key West Cheese Ball

Yield: 2 small cheese balls or 1 large cheese ball

½	pound sharp Cheddar cheese, shredded	2	tablespoons Worcestershire sauce
½	pound American cheese, shredded	1	teaspoon prepared mustard
8	ounces cream cheese	1	medium onion, chopped
2	tablespoons fresh lemon juice	½	cup grated Parmesan cheese
1	teaspoon garlic powder	½	cup paprika
½	cup mayonnaise		

- Combine the Cheddar, American and cream cheeses.

- Whisk the lemon juice, garlic powder, mayonnaise, Worcestershire sauce and mustard. Stir into the cheese mixture. Add onion and blend thoroughly.

- Form into 2 small balls or 1 large ball. Roll ball(s) in Parmesan cheese and then in paprika.

- Refrigerate, but do not freeze.

HOT CHILI FUDGE

Yield: approximately 4 dozen pieces

3	eggs, beaten	1	can chopped green chilies, drained (jalapeños if preferred)
2	cups shredded sharp Cheddar cheese		

- Preheat oven to 350 degrees. Spray an 8 x 8 x 2-inch baking dish with cooking spray.
- Combine the eggs, cheese and chilies mixing thoroughly.
- Bake for 30 minutes. Cut into 1-inch squares when cool.

PIQUANT CHEESE

SMITH & WELTON TEAROOM

Yield: 1½ cups

1	(10-ounce) package extra-sharp Cheddar cheese, grated	Dash of cayenne pepper
1	small onion, finely chopped	2-3 dashes of Worcestershire sauce
1	small green pepper, finely chopped	Ketchup

- Mix the cheese, onion and green pepper. Add cayenne pepper, Worcestershire sauce and enough ketchup to make the mixture spreadable, but not soupy.
- Serve with crackers or on toast points.

Burlie's Fresh Pimento Cheese

Yield: 4 sandwich servings or 1 cup

1	large, sweet pimento, finely chopped	½	cup shredded Cheddar cheese
1	large, ripe tomato, finely chopped	¼	cup mayonnaise
			Salt to taste
			Black pepper to taste

- Combine the pimento, tomatoes, cheese and mayonnaise. Season to taste with salt and pepper.

- Spread on sandwich bread or crackers.

Bring the fattened calf and kill it. Let's have a feast and celebrate.

Luke 15:23

Spinach-Bacon Deviled Eggs

Yield: 2 dozen

1	dozen hard-cooked eggs, peeled	2	tablespoons butter or margarine, softened
½	cup chopped fresh spinach	1	tablespoon sugar
¼	cup bacon, cooked and crumbled	1	teaspoon pepper
1	tablespoon apple cider vinegar	¼	teaspoon salt

- Slice eggs in half and scoop out the yolks. Mash the yolks in a bowl with a fork.

- Add the spinach, bacon, vinegar, butter or margarine, sugar, pepper and salt.

- Spoon the spinach mixture into the egg halves and chill for 1 hour.

Spinach Roll Ups

Yield: 8 to 10 servings

2	(10-ounce) packages frozen, chopped spinach	1	cup sour cream
½	(3¼-ounce) jar imitation bacon bits	1	(1-ounce) package ranch dressing mix
1	cup mayonnaise	1	bunch green onion, chopped
		8-10	(7½-inch) flour tortillas

- Defrost and squeeze water from spinach.
- Combine spinach with bacon bits, mayonnaise, sour cream, ranch dressing mix and green onions.
- Trim 2 sides of tortillas and spread 1 spoonful of spinach over each tortilla. Roll the tortilla up tightly and place in a plastic bag. Seal tightly. Refrigerate for 8 hours or you may freeze the rolls.
- Slice the tortilla rolls thinly and serve.

Shrimp Butter

Yield: 1½ cups

1	(3-ounce) package cream cheese	Juice of 1 lemon
½	cup butter	Salt to taste
2	(5-ounce) cans shrimp, drained	Parsley to garnish
1	tablespoon minced onion	

- Allow cream cheese and butter to reach room temperature and beat until smooth and creamy.
- Add shrimp, onion, lemon juice and salt. Beat thoroughly.
- Lightly butter the inside of a small bowl or mold. Pack the mixture into container and refrigerate until firm.
- Serve with crackers.

Shrimp Dip

Yield: 20 to 24 servings

1	(4¼-ounce) can tiny shrimp, drained	4	tablespoons mayonnaise
3	green onions, finely chopped	6	tablespoons grated Parmesan cheese
3	tablespoons sour cream		Dash white pepper

- Combine shrimp, onion, sour cream, mayonnaise and cheese. Season to taste with white pepper. Chill.
- Serve with crackers.

This recipe may easily be doubled.

Appetizers & Beverages

CHEF G'S SAHARA WRAP

TOURNAMENT PLAYER'S CLUB OF VIRGINIA BEACH

Yield: 2 to 4 servings

Wrap

2	herb tortillas	2	ounces Roma tomatoes, julienned
2	ounces hummus (recipe follows)	2	ounces hydroponic cucumber, julienned
4	ounces leaf lettuce, shredded		
1	ounce arugula, shredded	3	ounces feta cheese
6	ounces grilled chicken breast, julienned	2	ounces olive tapenade (recipe follows)

Hummus

2	ounces prepared hummus		Juice of ½ lemon
Pinch cumin		$^1/_2$	ounce extra virgin olive oil

Tapenade

4	ounces Kalamata olives, pitted		Pinch cumin
1	tablespoon dried oregano	½	ounce extra-virgin olive oil
1	tablespoon dried basil		Juice of ½ lemon

- For hummus combine hummus, cumin, lemon juice and olive oil. Mix well.

- For tapenade combine Kalamata olives, oregano, basil and cumin in a food processor.

- While processing, drizzle olive oil and lemon juice into mixture.

- Place tortillas on hot grill for approximately 5 seconds on each side.

- Spread hummus on heated tortillas, then place lettuce and arugula in the center. Add chicken, tomato, cucumber and feta cheese. Top with olive tapenade.

- Fold one side of the tortilla over the foodstuffs; fold the ends toward the center. Repeat this folding procedure until wrap looks like a burrito. Place toothpick in both ends of wraps and slice diagonally.

CAJUN SHRIMP

Yield: 25 appetizer servings

3	quarts water	1½	teaspoons salt
1	large lemon, sliced	1½	teaspoons seafood seasoning
4	pounds unpeeled shrimp	1½	teaspoons dried basil
½	cup olive oil	1½	teaspoons dried oregano
1½	cups vegetable oil	1½	teaspoons dried thyme
¼	cup hot pepper sauce	1½	teaspoons minced fresh parsley
1	tablespoon minced garlic		

■ Bring water and lemon slices to a boil.

■ Add shrimp and cook until pink, about 3 to 5 minutes. Drain shrimp and rinse with cold water. Chill.

■ Peel and devein chilled shrimp and place in a large, heavy-duty plastic storage bag.

■ Combine the olive oil, vegetable oil, hot pepper sauce, garlic, salt, seafood seasoning, basil, oregano, thyme and parsley. Mix thoroughly. Pour over shrimp in bag and seal. Marinate shrimp in refrigerator for 8 hours. Drain shrimp before serving.

This recipe may be made with half the shrimp.

HOT CRAB DIP

Yield: 8 to 12 servings

1	(8-ounce) package cream cheese, softened	1	teaspoon cream-style horseradish
1	tablespoon milk		Dash salt
8	ounces crabmeat		Dash pepper
3	tablespoons finely chopped onion		Slivered almonds

■ Preheat oven to 375 degrees.

■ Blend the cream cheese, milk and crabmeat. Stir in onion and horseradish. Season to taste with salt and pepper.

■ Spoon into an 8 x 8 x 2-inch baking dish. Sprinkle with sliced almonds.

■ Bake for 15 to 18 minutes. Serve hot with Melba toast or rye crackers.

CRAB TALBOT

Yield: 16 servings

1	stick butter	2	egg yolks, slightly beaten
6	tablespoons flour	½	cup sherry
4	cups light cream	1	pound crabmeat
⅔	tablespoon dry mustard	1	pound lobster meat
1	cup chopped mushrooms		Salt to taste
¾	cup Parmesan cheese, shredded		Pepper to taste

- Preheat oven to 350 degrees. Grease two 1-quart casserole dishes.

- Melt butter in a large skillet. Add flour slowly and stir until mixed and lightly brown. Add cream and whisk well, stirring until sauce begins to thicken. Whisk in dry mustard.

- When sauce is ready, add mushrooms, Parmesan cheese, egg yolks, sherry, lobster, crabmeat, salt and pepper to taste.

- Mix thoroughly and pour into casserole dishes. Bake for 20 to 30 minutes.

- Serve with toast points as either an entrée or appetizer.

SAUSAGE BALLS

Yield: 6 dozen

1	pound lean, hot sausage	1	(12-ounce) package shredded, sharp Cheddar cheese
3	cups baking mix		

- Preheat oven to 325 degrees.

- Knead the sausage, baking mix and cheese. Form into 1-inch balls and place on baking sheet.

- Bake for 20 to 30 minutes.

Champagne Royal

Yield: 12 servings

12 teaspoons Chambord or Crème de Cassis liqueur	2 (750-ml) bottles champagne, chilled Fresh strawberries or raspberries

- Pour a teaspoon of liqueur into 12 champagne flutes. Fill each with champagne. Place a fresh strawberry or several raspberries on the rim of the flute.
- The ingredients can be mixed and served from a punch bowl.

Coffee Punch

Yield: 24 servings

4 quarts whole milk	½ cup sugar
1 quart light cream	16 tablespoons instant coffee
2½ gallons coffee ice cream	

- Combine the milk, cream, ice cream, sugar and instant coffee. Mix thoroughly.
- Serve in small punch cups.

Fruit Punch

Yield: 20 servings

48 ounces cranberry juice	½ cup frozen lemon juice
12 ounces frozen orange juice	2 (28-ounce) bottles ginger ale, chilled

- Combine cranberry, orange and lemon juices in a punch bowl.
- Stir in the ginger ale. Mix thoroughly.

A frozen mold of berries can be floated in the punch to chill it. Recipe can be doubled.

Russian Tea

Yield: 16 servings

2	quarts water	5	tablespoons lemon juice
8	small teabags	1½	cups sugar
2½	cups orange juice		Whole cloves
2½	cups pineapple juice		

- Bring water to a boil. Add the tea bags and let stand for 15 minutes. Remove tea bags.

- Stir in orange juice, pineapple juice, lemon juice and sugar. Bring to a boil again and remove from the heat.

- Chill. Serve with 2 to 3 cloves in each cup.

Hot Buttered Rum

Yield: 25 servings

½	pound brown sugar	½	teaspoon cinnamon
½	pound confectioners' sugar	½	teaspoon nutmeg
½	pound butter		Rum
2	cups vanilla ice cream		Brandy
½	teaspoon allspice	25	cinnamon sticks

- Combine brown sugar, confectioners' sugar, butter, ice cream, allspice, cinnamon and nutmeg. Mix and cook over low heat, stirring often, until creamy.

- Cool mixture and refrigerate until ready to serve.

- Place 1 heaping tablespoon of the mixture into mug. Add 1 ounce of rum and 1 ounce of brandy. Fill the mug with boiling water and mix, stirring with a cinnamon stick. Sprinkle the top with nutmeg and serve.

Frosted Mocha Punch

Yield: 48 (4-ounce) servings

½ gallon vanilla ice cream, divided
⅔ cup instant freeze-dried coffee
¼ cup sugar
2 cups cold water

1 cup chocolate syrup
4 cups milk
1 cup heavy cream, whipped
1 (28-ounce) bottle club soda, chilled

■ Remove ice cream from freezer and spoon half into punch bowl to soften. Return rest of ice cream to freezer.

■ Measure coffee and sugar into a medium bowl. Stir in 2 cups cold water, stirring until coffee and sugar dissolve. Add chocolate syrup and milk to mixture. Pour over ice cream in punch bowl; stir until blended.

■ Fold in whipped cream and gently pour in club soda. Spoon remaining ice cream into punch and serve in 6-ounce punch cups.

Egg Nog

Yield: 20 servings

12 eggs, separated
2 cups sugar
Fifth of bourbon
1 pint light rum

1 pint heavy cream
1 pint whole milk
Nutmeg to garnish

■ Beat the egg yolks until light in color. Add sugar and beat until smooth and light.

■ Whip the cream.

■ Very slowly, add the bourbon, rum, whipped cream and milk to the egg yolk mixture.

■ When ready to serve, beat the egg whites until stiff and fold them into the egg nog. Sprinkle with nutmeg.

"Workers In The Field"
by David Freyss

Breakfast, Brunch & Bread

Breakfast, Brunch & Bread

Herbed Egg Casserole

Yield: 6 servings

2 cups herb-seasoned croutons	½ teaspoon dry mustard
1 cup shredded Cheddar cheese	⅛ teaspoon onion or garlic powder
4 eggs, slightly beaten	1 pound sausage, browned, drained and crumbled
2 cups milk	

■ Prepare this casserole the night before cooking.

■ Combine the croutons and cheese in the bottom of a greased 11 x 7 x 2-inch baking pan. Mix the eggs, milk, mustard and onion or garlic powder. Place the cooked sausage on top of the croutons and cheese. Pour the egg mixture over all. Refrigerate overnight.

■ Bring the casserole to room temperature before placing it in a preheated oven (set on counter for about an hour) or place the casserole in a cold oven and bake at 325 degrees for 45 to 50 minutes until browned and an inserted knife comes out clean.

Tarragon

Missouri Grits

Yield: 8 servings

1 cup uncooked grits	1 cup shredded Cheddar cheese
1 teaspoon salt	4 eggs, beaten
4 cups boiling water	1 cup milk
½ stick butter	

■ Preheat oven to 350 to 375 degrees and butter a 1½-quart baking dish.

■ Slowly pour grits and salt into boiling water, stirring so that no lumps form. Stir constantly for 2 to 5 minutes. Remove from heat, stir in butter and shredded cheese. Allow mixture to cool.

■ Mix eggs and milk into the grits and cheese mixture until thoroughly blended.

■ Bake uncovered in prepared dish for approximately 45 minutes until knife inserted in center comes out clean.

Breakfast Pizza

Yield: 12 servings

1	can of 8 crescent rolls	1½	cups frozen hash brown potatoes, thawed
7	eggs		
⅓	cup milk	1½	cups shredded sharp Cheddar cheese
½	teaspoon salt		
½	teaspoon pepper	2	tablespoons grated Parmesan cheese
1	pound sausage, browned, drained, and crumbled		

- Preheat oven to 325 degrees. Press rolls into an ungreased 9 x 13 x 2-inch baking dish.

- Whisk the eggs, milk, salt and pepper. Set aside. Spoon the cooked and drained sausage over the rolls, then spoon the hash browns over the sausage. Top with the shredded Cheddar cheese.

- Pour the egg mixture over the cheese. Sprinkle the Parmesan cheese on top. Bake for 25 minutes.

Hot Fruit Compote

Yield: 8 to 10 servings

1	(12-ounce) package pitted prunes	2	(10½-ounce) cans cherry pie filling
1	(6-ounce) package dried apricots	1	(11-ounce) can Mandarin oranges
1	(20-ounce) can pineapple chunks, drained	½	cup cooking sherry

- Preheat oven to 350 degrees. Lightly butter an oval or rectangular 9 x 13 x 2-inch baking dish.

- Layer prunes and apricots in bottom of prepared baking dish.

- Combine pineapple chunks, pie filling, oranges and sherry. Spoon mixture over the dried fruit.

- Bake uncovered for 1 hour.

This recipe compliments sausage and egg dishes as well as pork and poultry.

Corn Cakes

Yield: 3 to 4 servings

1 egg	1 teaspoon sugar
1½ cups buttermilk	1 teaspoon baking powder
2 tablespoons shortening	½ teaspoon baking soda
¾ cup white cornmeal	½ teaspoon salt
¼ cup all-purpose flour	

- Preheat griddle.

- Combine the eggs, buttermilk and shortening. Sift together the flour, sugar, baking powder, baking soda and salt. Add to egg mixture. Beat until batter is smooth.

- Drop by spoonfuls on a hot griddle. Serve with butter and syrup.

Pancake for Two

Yield: 2 servings

½ cup all-purpose flour	1 cup blueberries, well-drained
½ cup milk	
¼ teaspoon salt	¼ cup butter, margarine or vegetable cooking spray
2 eggs, beaten or comparable amount cholesterol-free real egg product	2 tablespoons lemon juice
	¼ cup confectioners' sugar

- Preheat oven to 450 degrees. Place iron skillet in oven.

- Blend flour, milk, salt and eggs. Fold in blueberries.

- Melt butter or margarine in iron skillet or spray skillet with vegetable cooking spray. Pour the batter into the very hot skillet.

- Bake 12 to 15 minutes. Remove from oven and sprinkle with lemon juice and confectioners' sugar. Cut in half and serve.

Best Ever Buttermilk Pancakes

Yield: 4 servings

"We have here only five loaves of bread and two fish."

Matthew 14:17

2	cups all-purpose flour	2	cups buttermilk
2	teaspoons baking powder	3	tablespoons melted butter
1	teaspoon salt	1	(10-ounce) can
½	teaspoon baking soda		blueberries, drained
2	eggs, well beaten		(optional)

- Combine flour, baking powder, salt and baking soda in a large bowl.

- In a small bowl, beat eggs and mix in the buttermilk and melted butter.

- By spoonfuls, stir buttermilk mixture into flour mixture. Batter will be lumpy. Stir in blueberries if desired.

- Cook in hot buttered skillet.

Morning Glory Muffins

Yield: 2 dozen

2	cups all-purpose flour	2	large cooking apples, peeled, cored and shredded
2	teaspoons baking soda		
½	teaspoon salt	¾	cup grated coconut
2	teaspoons ground cinnamon	½	cup raisins
1¼	cups sugar	½	cup chopped pecans
1½	cups finely shredded carrot	¾	cup vegetable oil
		3	eggs, slightly beaten
		½	teaspoon vanilla

- Preheat oven to 375 degrees.

- Grease or line muffin tins.

- Combine flour, soda, salt and cinnamon in a large bowl. Stir in sugar. Add carrots, apples, coconut, raisins and pecans. Stir well until coated. Make a well in the center of the mixture.

- In another bowl, combine the oil, eggs and vanilla. Add this to the dry ingredients, stirring until just moistened.

- Spoon the batter into muffin tins, filling ¾ full. Bake for 18-20 minutes or until golden brown.

Breakfast, Brunch & Bread

Sweet Potato Muffins

Christiana Campbell's Tavern

Yield: 2 dozen

1¼ cups plus 2 tablespoons sugar, divided
1¼ cups mashed sweet potatoes
1 stick butter, softened
2 large eggs
1½ cups all-purpose flour

1½ teaspoons ground cinnamon, divided
¼ teaspoon ground nutmeg
¼ teaspoon salt
1 cup milk
½ cup raisins
¼ cup chopped nuts

- Preheat oven to 400 degrees. Grease or line muffin tins.

- Combine 1¼ cups sugar with the mashed sweet potatoes and butter. Beat until smooth. Add the eggs.

- Sift together the flour, 1 teaspoon cinnamon, nutmeg and salt. Add to the potato mixture, alternating with milk. Add raisins and nuts. Spoon into muffin tins.

- Combine 2 tablespoons sugar with ½ teaspoon cinnamon. Sprinkle over the muffins and bake for 25 minutes.

The muffins may be frozen and reheated.

Pumpkin Chocolate Chip Muffins

Yield: 12 muffins

1⅔ cups all-purpose flour
1 cup sugar
1 teaspoon pumpkin pie spice
1 teaspoon cinnamon
1 teaspoon baking soda
¼ teaspoon baking powder

¼ teaspoon salt
2 large eggs
1 cup canned pumpkin
½ cup butter, melted
1 cup chocolate chips

- Preheat oven to 350 degrees. Grease muffin tin(s).

- Thoroughly mix flour, sugar, pie spice, cinnamon, baking soda, baking powder and salt in a large bowl.

- Beat eggs, pumpkin and butter. Pour over dry ingredients. Blend until just moistened. Mix chocolate chips into batter.

- Spoon mixture into muffin tins. Bake for 20 to 25 minutes.

Blueberry Muffins

WILLIAMSBURG INN

Yield: 2 dozen

1	stick butter	½	teaspoon salt
2	eggs	1	pinch baking soda
1⅛	cups sugar	1	tablespoon vanilla extract
3	cups all-purpose flour, plus	1	cup milk
	3 tablespoons	2	cups blueberries
3	teaspoons baking powder		

- Preheat oven to 400 degrees. Grease 2 muffin tins.

- Blend butter, eggs and sugar. Combine flour, baking powder, salt and baking soda, reserving 3 tablespoons flour.

- Add vanilla to milk and pour milk and flour mixture into butter and egg mixture. Mix well.

- Sprinkle 3 tablespoons of flour over blueberries. Fold berries into batter.

- Fill prepared muffin tins to ¾ full. Bake 15 to 20 minutes.

Blueberry Buttermilk Muffins

Yield: 1 dozen

2	cups all-purpose flour	1	egg, lightly beaten
½	cup sugar	1	cup buttermilk
2¼	teaspoons baking powder	¼	cup butter, melted
1	teaspoon salt	1	cup blueberries
¼	teaspoon baking soda		

- Preheat oven to 425 degrees. Grease a muffin tin.

- Combine flour, sugar, baking powder, salt and baking soda. Set aside. Stir egg, buttermilk and butter, mixing well.

- Make a well in the center of the dry ingredients. Pour in liquid ingredients and mix until dry ingredients are just moistened. Fold in blueberries.

- Fill prepared muffin tin ⅔ full. Bake for 20 to 30 minutes. Remove from pan immediately.

OATMEAL MUFFINS

Yield: 1 dozen muffins

1	cup rolled oats	1	cup less 2 tablespoons all-purpose flour
1	cup buttermilk		
⅓	cup safflower oil	1	teaspoon baking powder
¼	cup brown sugar	½	teaspoon baking soda
1	egg	1	teaspoon salt
1	tablespoon bran	¼-½	cup raisins, chopped dates or apples
1	tablespoon wheat germ		

▓ Soak oats in buttermilk for 1 hour.

▓ Preheat oven to 400 degrees. Grease or line a muffin tin.

▓ In a large bowl, mix oil, brown sugar and egg. In another bowl blend the bran, wheat germ, flour, baking powder, baking soda and salt. Alternating dry ingredients with buttermilk mixture, stir into the sugar mixture.

▓ Fold raisins, dates or apple bits into batter. Fill cups to ⅔ full and bake 20-25 minutes.

STRAWBERRY BREAD

Yield: 2 loaves, 16 servings

3	cups all-purpose flour	1¼	cups vegetable oil or ¾ cup vegetable oil plus ¾ cup orange juice
1	teaspoon salt		
1	teaspoon baking soda		
1	tablespoon cinnamon	2	(10-ounce) packages frozen strawberries or 3 cups fresh berries
2	cups sugar		
4	eggs, well beaten		
		1¼	cups chopped pecans

▓ Preheat oven to 350 degrees. Lightly grease two 9 x 5 x 3-inch loaf pans.

▓ Combine the flour, salt, baking soda, cinnamon and sugar. Mix the dry ingredients. Add eggs and oil or eggs, oil and orange juice, stirring only until moist.

▓ Fold in strawberries and pecans. Pour or spoon batter into prepared pans and bake for 1 hour or until done. Cool and let stand overnight before slicing.

CRANBERRY COFFEE CAKE

Yield: 12 to 16 servings

Cake

1	stick butter, softened	½	teaspoon salt
1	cup sugar	8	ounces sour cream
2	eggs	1	teaspoon almond extract
2	cups all-purpose flour	1	(16-ounce) can whole cranberry sauce
1	teaspoon baking powder		
1	teaspoon baking soda	½	cup chopped pecans

Almond Glaze

¾	cup confectioners' sugar	1	tablespoon warm water
½	teaspoon almond extract		

▓ Preheat oven to 350 degrees. Grease and flour a 10-inch tube pan.

▓ Blend butter and sugar. Add eggs one at a time and beat well after each addition.

▓ Combine flour, baking powder, baking soda and salt. Alternating dry ingredients with sour cream, beat into butter mixture. Stir in almond extract and mix well.

▓ Spoon ⅓ batter into prepared tube pan. Spread ⅓ cranberry sauce over batter. Repeat layers 2 more times, ending with a layer of cranberry sauce. Sprinkle pecans over the top.

▓ Bake 1 hour and cool thoroughly before icing with almond glaze.

▓ For glaze, mix confectioners' sugar, almond extract and warm water.

▓ Drizzle or spread over cranberry coffee cake.

Eat honey, my son, for it is good; honey from the comb is sweet to your taste. Know also that wisdom is sweet to your soul; if you find it, there is a future hope for you, and your hope will not be cut off.

Proverbs 24:13-14

Breakfast, Brunch & Bread

Lemon Bread

Yield: 1 loaf, 8 servings

½	cup butter	½	cup milk
1	cup sugar	½	cup chopped walnuts
2	eggs	1	tablespoon all-purpose flour
1¼	cups all-purpose flour plus 1 tablespoon, divided		Rind of 1 lemon, grated
1	teaspoon baking powder		Juice of 1 lemon
¼	teaspoon salt	¼	cup sugar

- Preheat oven to 350 degrees. Grease and flour a 9 x 5 x 3-inch loaf pan.

- Blend the butter and sugar until light and fluffy. Add the eggs.

- Sift 1¼ cups flour, baking powder and salt together. Add to the butter mixture gradually; alternately add the milk.

- Toss the walnuts in 1 tablespoon flour until nuts are coated. Fold these and the grated lemon rind into the batter and blend.

- Pour batter into the prepared loaf pan. Bake for 1 hour.

- Boil the lemon juice and ¼ cup sugar until sugar is dissolved. Pierce the top of the cooked bread in several places. Pour the hot syrup over the loaf and cool.

Be present at our table, Lord, Be here and everywhere adored. These creatures bless And grant that we May feast in Paradise with Thee. Amen.

Sautter Family Blessing from a book that belonged to Jane Sautter's great aunt

FRANKINCENSE

CRANBERRY WALNUT BREAD

Yield: 1 loaf, 8 servings

When all thy mercies, O my God! My rising soul surveys, Transported with the view, I'm lost In wonder, love and praise. Ten thousand thousand precious gifts Our daily thanks employ. Nor is the least a cheerful heart That tastes those gifts with joy. Amen.

Sautter Family Blessing

¼	cup vegetable oil	1½	teaspoons baking powder
½	cup low-fat buttermilk	2-3	tablespoons grated orange rind
1	cup sugar	¾	cup orange juice
1	egg	¾	cup walnut pieces
¼	cup egg substitute	1	cup fresh cranberries or ⅔ cup dried cranberries
2	cups all-purpose flour		
¼	teaspoon salt		

- Preheat oven to 350 degrees. Prepare a 9 x 5 x 3-inch loaf pan with cooking spray or lightly grease and flour.

- Combine oil, buttermilk, sugar and egg. Beat until thoroughly blended.

- In a separate bowl mix the flour, salt and baking powder. Slowly add to the egg mixture. With mixer on low, beat in the orange rind and juice.

- Fold in the cranberries and walnuts and pour batter into the prepared pan.

- Bake for 60 to 65 minutes or until cake tester inserted in the center comes out clean. Cool loaf in the pan for 10 minutes before removing.

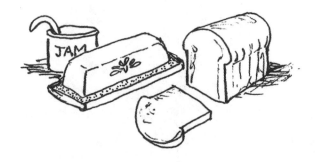

Mary Lou's Apricot Nut Loaf

Yield: 2 small loaves or 1 large loaf, 8 servings

1	cup dried apricots	1	cup sugar
2	cups all-purpose flour	1	egg, beaten
2	teaspoons baking powder	½	cup orange juice
½	teaspoon salt	¼	cup water
¼	teaspoon baking soda	½	cup chopped walnuts
¼	cup shortening		

- Preheat oven to 350 degrees and grease a 9 x 5 x 3-inch loaf pan or two 4½ x 2¾ x 1¼-inch loaf pans.

- Cut apricots into small pieces and soak in warm water for 15 minutes. Drain. Sift flour, baking powder, salt and baking soda together.

- In another bowl, blend the shortening and sugar. Beat in sifted ingredients, mixing thoroughly. Add egg, orange juice and water and mix. Fold in apricot pieces and walnuts.

- Pour batter into prepared loaf pans and bake for 60 minutes or until done. Cool for 10 minutes before removing from pan and cool thoroughly before slicing.

Freezes well.

Let your conversation be always full of grace, seasoned with salt, so that you may know how to answer everyone.

Colossians 4:6

*B*ANANA *B*READ

Yield: 1 loaf, 8 servings

1 stick butter or margarine	1 teaspoon vanilla
1 cup sugar	2 cups all-purpose flour
2 eggs, beaten	1 teaspoon baking soda
3 small or 2 large ripe bananas, mashed	Dash of salt
	1 cup chopped nuts (optional)

- Preheat oven to 275 degrees.

- Blend butter or margarine and sugar. Add eggs and mix, followed by the bananas and vanilla.

- In another bowl sift the flour, soda and salt. Add the dry ingredients to the banana mixture. Fold in the nuts.

- Pour batter into a 9 x 5 x 3-inch loaf pan and bake for 1½ hours.

*B*REAKFAST *S*TICKY *B*UNS

Yield: 6 to 8 servings

½ cup chopped pecans	¼ cup brown sugar
12 frozen rolls	¼ cup melted butter
½ (3-ounce) package instant butterscotch pudding	1 teaspoon cinnamon

- Grease and flour a 9 or 10-inch tube pan.

- Sprinkle pecans on bottom of prepared tube pan. Place frozen rolls on top of nuts. Sprinkle pudding mix over rolls.

- In a small bowl, combine the brown sugar, melted butter and cinnamon. Pour over the rolls. Cover with plastic wrap and let rolls rise overnight.

- The next morning, uncover and bake at 325 degrees for 30 minutes. Invert pan on a plate and serve.

Breakfast Cookies

Yield: 2 dozen servings

½	pound bacon	1	cup all-purpose flour
½	cup butter or margarine	¼	teaspoon baking soda
¾	cup sugar	2	cups corn flake cereal
1	egg	½	cup raisins (optional)

- Preheat oven to 350 degrees and grease a baking sheet.

- Fry bacon until crisp. Drain off grease and crumble.

- Combine butter and sugar. Beat in egg. Mix flour and baking soda. Stir into butter mixture.

- Fold in crumbled bacon, cereal and raisins.

- Drop by rounded teaspoons onto greased baking sheet. Bake for 15 to 18 minutes.

This is a great quick breakfast. The cookies can be baked ahead.

Bran Muffins

Yield: 6 dozen

4	eggs	3	teaspoons baking soda
1	cup butter or vegetable oil	4	tablespoons baking powder
1	quart buttermilk	2	teaspoons salt
2¼	cups sugar	1	(15-ounce) box wheat bran flakes
4¾	cups unsifted, all-purpose flour		cereal with raisins

- Preheat oven to 400 degrees.

- Combine eggs, butter and buttermilk in a large bowl. Stir in sugar, flour, baking soda, baking powder and salt. Fold in cereal.

- Pour batter into muffin tins and bake 15 to 25 minutes depending on size of muffin.

This batter will keep in the refrigerator 2 or 3 weeks.

Sour Cream Coffee Cake

Yield: 8 to 10 servings

Cake

¾	cup sugar	1	cup sour cream
1	stick butter	2	cups all-purpose flour
2	eggs	2	teaspoons baking powder
1	teaspoon vanilla extract	1	teaspoon baking soda

Filling

¼	cup granulated sugar	1	teaspoon cinnamon
¼	cup brown sugar	½-1	cup pecan pieces

- Preheat oven to 375 degrees. Grease and flour a 9-inch tube pan.

- For the batter, blend sugar and butter. Beat in eggs, vanilla and sour cream.

- Sift flour and baking soda together. Stir dry ingredients into sour cream mixture and mix well.

- For the filling, in a separate bowl combine granulated sugar, brown sugar, cinnamon and pecan pieces.

- Alternating between batter and filling, pour batter and filling mixture into the prepared pan. Bake for 35 minutes.

Buttermilk Biscuits

Yield: 10 biscuits

2	cups all-purpose flour	½	cup shortening
1	tablespoon sugar	¾	cup buttermilk or plain yogurt
2	teaspoons baking powder		Butter
½	teaspoon baking soda		

- Preheat oven to 400 degrees. Grease a baking sheet.

- In a large bowl combine flour, sugar, baking powder and baking soda. Cut in the shortening with one or two table knives until mixture is coarse and crumbly.

- Add the buttermilk or yogurt and stir until moistened and holds together. Do not over mix. If mixture is too sticky, add a little flour.

- Turn dough out onto a slightly floured surface and fold dough over itself about 4 times to create layers.

- Roll dough to ¾ inch thickness. Cut with a biscuit cutter. Place biscuits on baking sheet and brush tops with butter. Bake for 15 minutes until golden brown.

PUNGO BLUEBERRY FARM BISCUITS

Yield: 8 to 12 biscuits

Biscuits

2	cups all-purpose flour	⅓	cup butter-flavored
2	teaspoons baking powder		shortening
¼	teaspoon baking soda	1	large egg
½	cup sugar	¾	cup buttermilk
1	teaspoon salt	¼	cup fresh or frozen, thawed blueberries

Topping

3   tablespoons melted butter   ¼   teaspoon cinnamon
2   tablespoons sugar

- Preheat oven to 400 degrees. Grease a baking sheet.

- Combine flour, baking powder, baking soda, sugar and salt in a large bowl. Cut in the shortening with a pastry blender or knife until mixture is crumbly.

- Whisk egg and buttermilk and add to the flour mixture. By hand or using a mixer with dough prongs, mix until dough is moistened. Gently fold in the berries.

- Turn the dough onto a floured surface and knead 3 to 4 times. Roll out the dough to ¾-inch thickness. Cut with a 2 to 3-inch biscuit cutter and place on baking sheet.

- Bake for 15 minutes, or until golden brown.

- Stir melted butter, sugar and cinnamon. Brush the tops of biscuits with this mixture.

May use dehydrated buttermilk. Mix according to package.

So whether you eat or drink or whatever you do, do it all for the glory of God.

1 Corinthians 10:31

Myrnie's No-Fail Biscuits

Yield: 15 to 20 biscuits

⅓ cup vegetable oil
⅔ cup milk

2 cups self-rising flour

- ■ Preheat oven to 475 degrees.
- ■ Pour oil and milk into flour at the same time. With a fork, stir dough until sides of the bowl are clean. Smooth dough by kneading it about 10 times.
- ■ Without using additional flour, press or roll the dough between waxed paper until it is ¼-inch thick, or for thicker biscuits, ½-inch thick. Cut biscuits with an unfloured biscuit cutter.
- ■ Bake for 10 to 12 minutes.

For 8 to 10 biscuits use 1 cup self-rising flour and ⅓ cup milk filled to ½ cup with vegetable oil.

Skillet Corn Bread

Yield: 8 servings

2-3 teaspoons bacon drippings
2 cups buttermilk
1 large egg
1¾ cups cornmeal

1 teaspoon baking powder
1 teaspoon baking soda
1 teaspoon salt

- ■ Preheat oven to 450 degrees. Coat the bottom and sides of a 10-inch iron skillet with bacon drippings. Heat skillet in oven.
- ■ Whisk the buttermilk and egg. Stir in cornmeal, baking powder, baking soda and salt. Mix well.
- ■ Pour batter into hot skillet. Bake for 15 to 20 minutes or until golden.

BEER CORN BREAD

Yield: 9 to 12 servings

1	cup yellow cornmeal	½	cup milk
1	cup all-purpose flour	1	cup lager beer
½	cup corn kernels, canned or frozen and thawed	1	tablespoon butter, melted
4	teaspoons baking powder	½	cup shredded Cheddar cheese
2	tablespoons chopped green onions	1	egg, beaten

- Preheat oven to 425 degrees. Grease an 8 x 8-inch baking dish.

- Mix cornmeal, flour, corn kernels, baking powder and green onion.

- Stir in milk, beer, butter, cheese and egg. Mix well. Pour into prepared baking dish.

- Bake for 20 minutes.

Jean Ford recommends serving this recipe with chili.

CREAM STYLE CORN MUFFINS

Yield: 6 to 8 muffins

1	cup self-rising flour	3	eggs, beaten
1	cup sour cream	1	teaspoon salt
1	(15½-ounce) can creamed corn		

- Preheat oven to 350 degrees. Grease a small muffin tin and place in oven to heat.

- Mix the flour, sour cream, corn, eggs and salt. Pour batter into hot tins. Bake 12 to 15 minutes.

Corn Sticks or Muffins

Yield: 3 dozen

1½ cups cornmeal
½ cup flour
1 teaspoon sugar
1 teaspoon salt
1 tablespoon baking powder

2 eggs, slightly beaten
½ teaspoon baking soda
1½ cups buttermilk
½ cup melted butter, divided

- Preheat oven to 400 degrees. Place iron corn stick mold or muffin tins in the oven to heat.

- Mix the cornmeal, flour, sugar, salt and baking powder. Pour in the eggs, buttermilk, baking soda and half the butter. Stir until mixture is evenly moist.

- Brush the hot molds or tins with remaining butter. Fill about ½ full with batter.

- Cook for 10 minutes or until brown and crusty.

Deluxe Cornbread

Yield: 16 servings

1 cup sour cream
½ cup olive oil
1 (15-ounce) can creamed corn
1 cup cornmeal

1½ teaspoons salt
3 teaspoons baking powder
2 eggs, beaten

- Preheat oven to 375 degrees. Grease an 8 x 8 x 2-inch baking dish.

- In a mixing bowl, combine sour cream, oil, corn, cornmeal, salt and baking powder. Stir in eggs.

- Pour batter into prepared baking dish. Bake for 40 minutes.

"Cuke" Elmore's Hush Puppies

Yield: 3 dozen

1 cup cornmeal	½ cup buttermilk
1 teaspoon baking powder	1 egg
½ teaspoon salt	1 large onion, minced
1 teaspoon sugar	Oil for frying

- Combine the cornmeal, baking powder, salt and sugar. Pour in buttermilk and egg. Add onion and mix well. Add water if batter is too stiff.

- Drop by spoonfuls into hot oil. Cook until golden brown.

Mother's Spoon Bread

Yield: 4 servings

2 cups boiling water	2 teaspoons salt
1 cup cornmeal	1 teaspoon butter
1 cup milk	1 tablespoon sugar
2 eggs, beaten	

- Preheat oven to 325 degrees. Grease a 1½-quart baking dish.

- Pour boiling water over cornmeal and let it stand for a few minutes. Stir in milk, eggs, salt, butter and sugar. Mix well. Spoon into prepared baking dish.

- Bake for 1 hour.

SALLY LUNN BREAD

Yield: 12 servings

1	cup milk, scalded	1	(¼-ounce) package rapid-rise yeast
½	cup butter, sliced		
4¼	cups water, divided	3	eggs, beaten
¼	cup sugar	4	cups all-purpose flour
1	teaspoon salt	Butter	

- Scald the milk by heating in microwave for 2 minutes. Place slices of butter in the scalded milk and set aside to cool.

- Pour ¼ cup warm water in a mixing bowl. Stir in sugar, salt and yeast. Add milk and butter and then eggs. Gradually beat in flour by hand or with electric mixer with dough hook. A bread machine can be used.

- Warm the oven to 140 degrees. Place the dough in a greased bowl and cover with plastic wrap. Boil 2 cups water and sit in warm oven. Turn oven off and put dough in oven with boiled water. Leave dough in oven for 1 to 1½ hours, until it has doubled in size.

- Grease a 10-inch tube pan. Transfer the risen dough to the prepared tube pan. Cover again with plastic wrap and place in a warm oven with 2 more cups of boiling water. Allow another 1 to 1½ hours for dough to rise. Remove plastic wrap and water.

- Set oven at 200 degrees and gradually increase the oven heat 5 degrees every 5 minutes until oven temperature reaches 325 degrees. This prevents the dough from sinking.

- Cook for about 45 minutes. Cool 5 minutes, then turn upside down on a plate. Brush with butter or shortening.

Take wheat and barley, beans and lentils, millet and spelt; put them in a storage jar and use them to make bread for yourself.

Ezekiel 4:9

WHOLE WHEAT HERB AND ONION BREAD

Yield: 2 loaves

2	cups milk	½	cup wheat germ
3	tablespoons butter, melted	½	small onion, minced
		1	teaspoon rosemary
1	tablespoon salt	½	teaspoon dill weed
3	tablespoons honey	½	teaspoon thyme
2	tablespoons dry yeast	5½-6	cups whole-wheat flour, divided
⅓	cup lukewarm water		

- Preheat oven to 140 degrees. Butter a 2-quart bowl.

- Scald milk in a saucepan or by heating on high in microwave for 3 minutes. In a large bowl, combine milk, butter, salt and honey. Cool.

- Dissolve yeast in water. Add yeast to the milk and honey mixture. Stir in wheat germ, onion, rosemary, dill weed, thyme and 3 cups of flour. Stir vigorously with wooden spoon or mix with a dough hook or in a bread machine until smooth. Gradually add more flour until dough is too stiff to stir.

- If not using a dough hook or bread machine, turn dough out onto floured board. Knead until smooth and elastic. Place dough in buttered bowl. Cover and place in a warm oven, about 140 degrees. Allow dough to rise until double in size, about 1 hour.

- Punch dough down, cover and let rise again. Knead dough a few more times and place in two 9 x 5 x 3-inch loaf pans. Let rise 45 minutes.

- Preheat oven to 375 degrees and bake for 45 minutes.

Still other seed fell on good soil, where it produced a crop—a hundred, sixty or thirty times what was sown.

Matthew 13:8

Rosemary

DILLY BREAD

Yield: 1 loaf or 6 to 8 servings

1	(¼-ounce) package yeast	2	teaspoons dill seed
¼	cup lukewarm water	1	teaspoon salt
1	cup cottage cheese	¼	teaspoon baking soda
2	tablespoons sugar	1	egg
1	tablespoon dried minced onion	2½	cups sifted flour
1	tablespoon butter		

■ Dissolve yeast in water. Combine cottage cheese, sugar, onion, butter, dill seed, salt, baking soda, egg and yeast in a mixing bowl. Gradually beat in flour to form stiff dough by hand or use a bread machine. Cover dough and let it rise in a warm place until doubled, 50 to 60 minutes.

■ Stir dough down and place into a well-greased 1½ to 2-quart baking dish. Let dough rise again until light, another 30 to 40 minutes.

■ Preheat oven to 325 degrees. Bake 45 to 50 minutes until golden brown. Brush with butter and sprinkle with salt.

EASY POPOVERS

Yield: 8 to 10 popovers

1	cup milk	½	teaspoon salt
1	cup flour	3	eggs
3	tablespoons melted butter or vegetable oil		

■ Preheat oven to 400 degrees. Place muffin tins in oven for at least 10 minutes.

■ Blend milk, flour, butter, salt and eggs in a blender.

■ Pour batter into hot muffin tins, filling each cup about ⅔ full.

■ Bake for 15 minutes. Reduce oven temperature to 360 degrees and continue baking for 30 minutes more. *Do not open the oven door while popovers are cooking.*

■ Serve immediately while piping hot.

Irvin Gentry's Dinner Rolls

Yield: Approximately 3 dozen

2	(¼-ounce) packages dry yeast	2	cups scalded milk (125-130 degrees)
½	cup sugar	2	eggs (at room temperature)
1	tablespoon salt		
4	tablespoons vegetable shortening	6-7	cups all-purpose flour, divided

- Blend yeast, sugar, salt, and 3 cups flour in a large mixing bowl. Beat in shortening and hot milk, mixing thoroughly until the batter is smooth.

- Lightly beat eggs and stir into the batter. Beat 100 strokes. Gradually add remaining flour until the dough forms a large ball and sides of the bowl are clean. Turn dough onto a floured surface and knead until dough is smooth and elastic. Add small amounts of flour if dough is too sticky, but do not add so much flour that the dough is easy to handle. The dough should be soft.

- Place dough in a greased bowl covered with plastic wrap. Allow dough to rise at room temperature until it has doubled in size, about 1 hour.

- Punch down the dough and shape pieces as desired for rolls. Place these on a prepared baking sheet to rise again. Cover with a cloth. They will double in size in 45 to 60 minutes. Cover rolls with a cloth while they rise.

- Preheat oven to 400 degrees. Bake rolls for 10 to 12 minutes until golden brown. Unused dough can be covered and stored in the refrigerator for up to 1 week.

- An easy baking method is to place two 1-inch dough balls in each cup of a greased muffin tin and let them rise and bake as above.

To Thee, O Lord, our hearts we raise, For mercies marking all our days. Each morn our wants are satisfied With food Thy love and care provide. Amen.

Sautter Family Blessing

Hardy's Famous Hot Rolls

Yield: approximately 2½ dozen

1⅓ cups warm water
⅓ cup sugar
1 tablespoon salt
2 (¼-ounce) packages rapid-rise dry yeast
4 eggs, well beaten
1 stick butter-flavored shortening or butter, divided
5⅓ cups all-purpose flour
4 cups boiling water, divided

- Warm the oven to about 140 degrees and turn it off. Grease a bowl large enough for the dough to double in size.

- Place warm water in a large mixing bowl. Mix sugar, salt, yeast, eggs and ⅓ cup shortening with the water using an electric mixer with a dough hook or bread machine.

- Gradually add flour and beat until dough is smooth.

- Place the dough into the prepared bowl and cover with plastic wrap. Place the bowl of dough and 2 cups of boiling water in the warm oven. Leave for 1 to 1½ hours or until dough has doubled in size.

- Knead the dough on a floured surface, sprinkling a little flour on top. Roll dough to ⅜-inch thickness.

- Cut dough with a large biscuit cutter. Place a small amount of butter-flavored shortening or butter on top and fold dough over.

- Warm oven to about 140 degrees again and turn off. Place rolls on a 17¼ x 11½ x 2¼-inch greased roasting pan, 3 across and 9 down. Leave space between for rolls to rise. Cover with plastic wrap and place in the warm oven with 2 cups of boiling water. Allow rolls to rise again until they double in size, about 1 hour.

- Remove rolls from oven and uncover. Preheat oven to 350 degrees.

- Bake for 15 minutes, until golden brown. Brush with melted butter or shortening.

Breakfast, Brunch & Bread

"The Chef"
by Sara Moore

Soups, Salads & Dressings

Soups, Salads & Dressings

Cold Beet Soup

Yield: 3 cups

1	(15-ounce) can sliced beets	Dash garlic powder	
1	cup buttermilk	Minced parsley	
1/8	teaspoon onion salt		

- Place beets, buttermilk, onion salt and garlic powder into blender. Process at high speed until smooth.
- Cover and refrigerate until chilled. Garnish with parsley and serve.

Cold Zucchini Soup

Yield: 9 servings

4	medium zucchini, cut into chunks	2	(8-ounce) packages cream cheese, softened
4	cups chicken broth		
1	bunch green onions, chopped	1	tablespoon fresh dill
1	teaspoon pepper	8	ounces sour cream
1	teaspoon salt	Chopped fresh chives	

- Combine zucchini, broth, onions, pepper and salt in a large saucepan. Cook over medium-high heat, stirring occasionally, for 20 minutes. Cut softened cream cheese into chunks. Add cream cheese and dill to zucchini mixture.
- Process the soup in batches in blender until smooth. Cover and refrigerate for 8 hours. Stir in sour cream and garnish with chives before serving.

Chilled Cucumber Soup

Yield: 4 servings

1¼	cups undiluted cream of chicken soup	Dash curry powder
½	cup milk	Dash dried onion
1	cucumber, peeled and cut into pieces	Salt
		Pepper
8	ounces sour cream	Fresh chives

- Combine the soup, milk, cucumber, sour cream, curry powder, onion, salt and pepper in a blender. Blend well.
- Chill until ready to serve. Top with chopped chives.

Sis's Gazpacho

Yield: 8 to 10 servings

4   large tomatoes, peeled and chopped or 1 (14½-ounce) can tomatoes
1   medium onion, chopped
1   clove garlic, minced
1   green pepper, seeded and chopped
1   large cucumber, peeled and chopped

1   cup vegetable or tomato juice
½   tablespoon wine vinegar
2   teaspoons salt
¼   teaspoon pepper
Sour cream

■ In a blender or food processor, combine the tomatoes, onion, garlic, green pepper and cucumber. Process briefly and add vegetable or tomato juice, vinegar, salt and pepper. Process a few more seconds until the soup is the desired consistency.

■ Chill and serve with a dollop of sour cream.

Sliced olives may be used as a garnish also.

Suzanne's Gazpacho

Yield: 4 servings or 6 to 8 appetizer servings

1   clove garlic, minced
½   small onion, sliced
½   green pepper, seeded and sliced
3   ripe tomatoes, peeled and quartered or 1 (14½-ounce) can whole peeled tomatoes
1   small cucumber, peeled and quartered

1   teaspoon salt
¼   teaspoon pepper
3   tablespoons olive oil
3   tablespoons wine vinegar
½   cup tomato juice
Croutons, green pepper or green onion

■ Place garlic, onion, green pepper, tomatoes, cucumber, salt, pepper, olive oil, vinegar and tomato juice into a blender. Process for 3 seconds or until all the cucumber has been blended.

■ Chill. Serve with croutons and chopped green pepper or chopped green onion as garnish.

Soups, Salads & Dressings

Nancy's Gazpacho

Yield: 6 servings

30 ounces Bloody Mary mix, divided	1 cucumber, halved and chopped, divided
⅓ cup canola oil	
¼ cup balsamic vinegar	1 tomato, halved and chopped, divided

- Place 10 ounces Bloody Mary mix, oil, vinegar, half the cucumber and half the tomato in a blender. Blend until smooth.

- In a large bowl mix 20 ounces Bloody Mary mix with remaining chopped cucumber and tomato. Stir in the processed mixture. Chill.

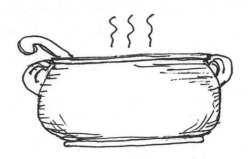

Tomato-Cucumber Soup

Yield: 6 cups

3 medium cucumbers, peeled, seeded and chopped	1 cup chicken broth
3 medium tomatoes, cored, seeded and chopped	16 ounces sour cream
	½ teaspoon salt
1 teaspoon minced garlic	½ teaspoon ground black pepper
½ cup sliced onions or scallions	Cucumber slices (optional)
¼ cup snipped fresh parsley	Cherry or grape tomato wedges (optional)
3 tablespoons cider vinegar	

- In a blender or food processor, add the cucumbers, tomatoes, garlic, onions, parsley and vinegar. Cover and process until nearly smooth. If using a blender, blend half the vegetables at a time. Transfer purée to a bowl. Stir in chicken broth.

- Serve immediately or cover and chill up to 4 hours. Before serving, add sour cream and whisk until smooth. Stir in salt and pepper. If desired, garnish with cucumber and tomato.

Carrot and Orange Soup

Yield: 4 servings

2	pounds carrots, cleaned and sliced		Pepper
1	large onion, chopped	1	bay leaf
1	ounce butter or margarine		Juice of 2 oranges
2	pints chicken stock or chicken broth		Heavy cream, partially whipped
Salt			

- In a large stockpot, sauté carrots and onion in butter or margarine until onion is soft. Add the stock or broth, salt, pepper and bay leaf. Simmer until carrots are tender. Remove from heat; let cool and remove the bay leaf. Return to the heat and add orange juice.

- Purée ½ or more of the soup in a blender for a creamier texture. Serve hot with a swirl of whipped cream on top.

Cheddar Broccoli Chowder

Yield: 8 servings

2	tablespoons butter	3	cups finely chopped broccoli florets (may also use carrots and cauliflower)
1	small onion, finely chopped		
¼	cup flour	1½	cups milk
3	cups vegetable or chicken stock	1½	cups shredded Cheddar cheese
2	cups peeled and cubed potatoes		Freshly ground pepper
1	bay leaf		

- In a large stockpot melt butter over medium heat. Add onions and stir for 2 minutes or until tender. Blend in flour. Add stock and bring to a boil, stirring until mixture thickens.

- Add potatoes and bay leaf. Reduce heat, cover and simmer for 10 minutes, stirring occasionally. Add broccoli and simmer for 10 minutes until vegetables are tender.

- Stir in milk and cheese. Heat until cheese is melted and soup is piping hot. Be careful not to let it boil. Remove bay leaf and season with pepper to taste.

Yellow Squash Soup

Yield: 4 servings

2	pounds yellow squash		Pinch crushed red pepper
2	cups chicken broth or 4 chicken bouillon cubes plus 2 cups boiling water	3	ounces cream cheese

■ Cut squash into medium-sized pieces. Cook in broth (or bouillon) until soft. Add red pepper. Add cream cheese.

■ Pour cooked squash mixture with liquid into blender. Purée soup in batches. Heat and serve.

Aunt Jac's Zucchini Soup

Yield: 2 to 3 quarts

2	cups chopped onions	2	cups chicken broth
¼	cup plus 2 tablespoons melted butter	¼	teaspoon pepper
4	cups diced yellow squash, zucchini and broccoli	1	teaspoon celery salt
		½	teaspoon dried tarragon
		2	cups milk

■ Sauté onions in melted butter until golden. Add squash, zucchini, broccoli, broth, pepper, celery salt and tarragon. Cook until tender.

■ Remove from heat and add milk. Fill the blender half full and blend until creamy. Repeat until all has been processed.

■ Serve soup hot.

Freezes well.

Butternut Squash Soup

Yield: 6 servings

4 cups peeled and diced butternut squash
2 chopped onions
1 quart or more chicken broth
1-2 Granny Smith apples, peeled and chopped
Dash Worcestershire sauce

Dash lemon juice
1-2 teaspoons balsamic vinegar (optional)
½ teaspoon curry powder
Salt
Crystallized ginger, slivered

- Bake, boil or microwave squash until done.

- Boil onions in broth and add squash. Add apples. Cook a few minutes more.

- Season with Worcestershire sauce, lemon juice, vinegar, curry powder and salt.

- Purée in blender, adding more chicken broth if soup is too thick. Serve hot, garnished with ginger.

Pumpkin Soup

Yield: 8 servings

2 tablespoons butter
1 medium onion, chopped
1 (16-ounce) can pumpkin
2½ cups chicken stock
1 (10¾-ounce) can cream of chicken soup

⅔ cup half-and-half
¼ teaspoon paprika
Salt
Pepper
Sour cream

- Melt butter in a large saucepan. Cook onions in butter until soft. Add canned pumpkin and stock. Bring to a boil. Simmer 30 minutes. Add chicken soup.

- Pour into blender. Process mixture until puréed. Return purée to a clean pan and stir in the half-and-half. Season with paprika, salt and pepper. Reheat slowly.

- Serve with a small dollop of sour cream on top.

Black-Eyed Pea Soup

Yield: 8 servings

1	medium onion, chopped	2-3 bouillon cubes
½	pound butternut squash, seeded and chopped	4-5 cups water
		Freshly ground pepper
1	medium turnip, chopped	1½ tablespoons brown rice vinegar
2	parsnips, chopped (optional)	1 tablespoon ume plum vinegar
2	tablespoons canola oil	1 tablespoon finely chopped green onions
2	(15-ounce) cans black-eyed peas, rinsed	

■ Sauté onion, squash, turnip and parsnips in oil until soft. Add black-eyed peas and bouillon cubes dissolved in the water. Simmer 20 minutes. Add pepper and vinegars in the last 10 minutes.

■ Purée 2 cups of soup in blender and pour back into soup. This will give the soup a creamy consistency.

■ Pour in soup bowls and garnish with green onions. Serve with French bread or corn bread.

Mimi's Vegetarian Chili

Yield: 6 to 8 servings

2	green peppers, seeded and diced	2 tablespoons chili powder
1	medium onion, chopped	2 (15-ounce) cans pinto beans
1	zucchini, chopped	2 (15-ounce) cans black beans
1	yellow squash, chopped	2 (14½-ounce) cans stewed tomatoes
1	(4-ounce) can chopped chili peppers	

■ Sauté the green peppers and onions until tender.

■ Add the zucchini, squash, chili peppers, chili powder, pinto beans, black beans and tomatoes. Simmer for 30 to 40 minutes, stirring often.

Freezes well.

PASTA E FAGIOLI

Yield: 4 servings

1½ teaspoons olive oil	½ teaspoon rosemary
1 cup chopped onions	1 (15-ounce) can great Northern beans
1 clove garlic, minced	1 (14½-ounce) can diced tomatoes
2 ribs celery, chopped	4 cups chicken broth
2 carrots, chopped	⅓ cup small pasta (ditalini, if possible)
2 tablespoons parsley	Olive oil
½ teaspoon basil	Parmesan cheese

- Heat oil, add onions, garlic, celery, carrots, parsley, basil and rosemary. Cook covered until carrots soften, about 10 minutes. Slightly crush beans as they are added. Stir in tomatoes and chicken broth. Bring to boil. Add pasta and simmer until pasta is cooked.

- Add more chicken broth if soup is too thick.

- Garnish with olive oil and Parmesan cheese.

Leftover soup improves when pasta is cooked separately al dente, then added to soup.

NOODLE CHILI

Yield: 10 servings

2 pounds ground round, chicken or turkey	1 bay leaf
3 tablespoons olive oil	½ teaspoon ground cumin
1 (28-ounce) can tomatoes	½ teaspoon oregano
4 cups tomato juice	½ teaspoon pepper
2 cups chopped onion	1 (15-ounce) can kidney beans
3 cloves garlic, minced	1 cup chopped sweet pickle
4 teaspoons salt	2 cups thin egg noodles, cooked and drained
2 tablespoons chili powder	

- Brown meat in olive oil and stir until crumbly. Pour off liquid or grease. Add tomatoes, tomato juice, onion, garlic, salt, chili powder, bay leaf, cumin, oregano and pepper. Mix well, cover and simmer for 1 hour.

- Stir in kidney beans and pickle. Cook for 30 minutes. Add the cooked noodles.

Soups, Salads & Dressings

White Bean Chili

Yield: 12 (1-cup) servings

1	pound dried or 4 (15-ounce) cans great Northern beans	6	cups chicken broth
1	tablespoon olive oil	5	cups cooked chicken breast, cubed
2	medium onions, chopped	12	ounces Monterey Jack cheese, shredded and divided
2	teaspoons ground cumin	½	teaspoon salt
1½	teaspoons dried oregano	½	teaspoon pepper
	Dash red pepper	¾	cup sour cream
2	(4½-ounce) cans chopped green chilies, drained	¾	cup salsa
4	cloves garlic, minced		Chopped fresh parsley (optional)

- If using dried beans, soak overnight or 8 hours. Drain and rinse beans.

- Heat olive oil in Dutch oven over medium high heat. Sauté onion until tender. Add cumin, oregano, red pepper, green chilies and garlic.

- Add beans and broth. Bring to a boil, cover and reduce heat. Simmer, stirring occasionally for about 10 minutes. Add the chicken, 1 cup of cheese, salt and pepper. Bring to a boil. Reduce the heat and simmer uncovered for 10 minutes, stirring frequently. If using dried beans, check for tenderness.

- Spoon into bowls. Top with sour cream, remaining cheese and salsa.

Above all, love each other deeply, because love covers over a multitude of sins. Offer hospitality to one another without grumbling. Each one should use whatever gift he has received to serve others, faithfully administering God's grace in its various forms.

1 Peter 4:8-10

Spicy Hot Chili

Yield: 15 to 20 servings

1	pound hot sausage	1	(28-ounce) can tomato sauce
3	pounds ground round	1	tablespoon salt
3	large onions, diced	1	tablespoon oregano
6	cloves garlic, minced	¼	cup red wine
4	tablespoons chili powder	1	tablespoon brown sugar
2	tablespoons flour	3	(15-ounce) cans kidney beans
3	bay leaves		Sour cream (optional)
2	(28-ounce) cans tomatoes		Shredded sharp Cheddar cheese
1	(15-ounce) can tomatoes		(optional)

■ Brown sausage and ground round in a large stockpot. Add onions and garlic; sauté for 10 minutes.

■ Add chili powder, flour, bay leaves, tomatoes, tomato sauce, salt, oregano, red wine and brown sugar. Cook on low for 4 hours or medium-low for 2 hours. Add kidney beans and cook another 15 minutes.

■ Serve with a dollop of sour cream and shredded cheese.

Alice Reuger Circle's Cabbage Soup

Yield: 8 to 10 servings

1	pound ground beef	1	(14½-ounce) can carrots, drained
1	(46-ounce) can tomato juice	2	(15-ounce) cans kidney beans,
2	(28-ounce) cans tomatoes		rinsed and drained
1	small head cabbage, chopped		Salt
1	large green pepper, seeded and		Pepper
	chopped		Garlic powder
1	onion, chopped	2	dashes hot pepper sauce

■ Brown and drain the beef. Set aside. In a large stockpot combine the tomato juice, tomatoes, cabbage, green pepper and onion. Cook until tender.

■ Add the ground beef, carrots, beans, salt, pepper, garlic powder and hot pepper sauce. Cook until hot.

Bishop Gunn Circle's Lenten Luncheon Soup

Yield: 16 servings

1	pound ground beef
4	medium white potatoes, peeled and cubed
1	large onion, diced
1	(16-ounce) bag frozen mixed vegetables

2-3 (46-ounce) cans vegetable juice, divided
1 cup beef bouillon or broth
½ head cabbage, shredded

◼ Brown and drain ground beef. Combine beef, potatoes, onion, mixed vegetables, 2 cans vegetable juice, beef bouillon (or broth) and cabbage in a large stockpot.

◼ Simmer for 2 hours. Add the additional vegetable juice if soup becomes too thick.

Bay

Lenten Luncheon Vegetable Beef Soup

Yield: 8 servings

3   pounds stew beef
2   (18-ounce) cans tomato juice
⅓   cup chopped onion
4   teaspoons salt
2   teaspoons Worcestershire sauce
¼   teaspoon chili powder
2   bay leaves
6   cups water

1   (10-ounce) package frozen lima beans
1   (14½-ounce) can tomatoes
1   cup diced celery
1   (8¾-ounce) can whole kernel corn
1   cup sliced carrots
1   cup diced potatoes

◼ Brown the stew beef in a skillet. Combine the browned beef, tomato juice, onion, salt, Worcestershire sauce, chili powder and bay leaves in a large stockpot. Add water, cover and simmer for 2 hours.

◼ Add lima beans, tomatoes, celery, corn, carrots and potatoes. Cover and simmer for 1 more hour before serving.

VEAL STEW

Yield: 4 servings

1-1½	pounds veal, cubed	1½	cups chicken broth or white wine
3	tablespoons olive oil		Generous pinch oregano
1	small onion, chopped		Generous pinch parsley
2	large cloves garlic, chopped		Juice of 1 lemon, divided
1	tablespoon flour	1	pound large white mushrooms,
1	(10-ounce) can diced tomatoes		quartered

■ Sauté veal in oil until browned. Transfer to a 2½ or 3-quart saucepan.

■ Add onions and garlic to original pan and sauté. Sprinkle with flour and cook for 2 minutes.

■ Transfer to saucepan with veal. Add tomatoes, chicken broth or wine, oregano, parsley and half the lemon juice.

■ Simmer 1½ hours. Add mushrooms and cook for 30 minutes longer. Before serving, add remaining lemon juice. Serve over brown or wild rice.

SKIERS' CHOWDER

Yield: 8 servings

1	pound hot pork sausage	1½	teaspoons seasoned salt
2	(15-ounce) cans kidney beans	½	teaspoon garlic salt
1	(28-ounce) can tomatoes, broken up	½	teaspoon thyme
1	quart water	⅛	teaspoon pepper
1	large onion, chopped	1	cup diced potatoes
1	bay leaf	½	green pepper, chopped

■ Cook sausage until brown and drain thoroughly. In a large stockpot combine the kidney beans, tomatoes, water, onion, bay leaf, seasoned salt, garlic salt, thyme and pepper. Add the sausage, cover and simmer 1½ hours.

■ Add potatoes and green pepper. Cover and cook for 15 to 20 minutes more until potatoes are tender. Remove bay leaf and serve.

CHICKEN AND SAUSAGE FILÉ GUMBO

Yield: 16 servings

⅔	cup vegetable oil	1	tablespoon finely minced garlic
1	(3½ to 4-pound) fryer, cut up	2	cups chopped onion
½	cup flour	2	quarts cold water, divided
1¼	pounds smoked sausage, sliced into ½-inch thick pieces	3	teaspoons salt
		1	teaspoon freshly ground black pepper
½	pound lean baked ham, cubed	⅛	teaspoon cayenne pepper
½	chopped green pepper		
½	cup finely chopped green onion tops	1¼	teaspoons dried thyme
2	tablespoons finely minced parsley	3	whole bay leaves, crushed
		2½-3	tablespoons filé powder

■ Preheat oven to 175 degrees.

■ Heat oil in a 7 to 8-quart stockpot over high heat. Brown chicken pieces and remove to heated platter. Place in oven to keep warm.

■ Gradually add flour to the heated oil, reduce heat and stir constantly until the roux is medium brown. Immediately add sausage, ham, green pepper, green onion tops, parsley, garlic and onion. Continue cooking and stirring over low heat for 10 minutes more.

■ Add ¼ cup water, reserved chicken pieces, salt, black pepper, cayenne pepper, thyme and bay leaves; mix thoroughly. Gradually stir in the rest of the water. Raise heat and bring to a boil, then lower the heat and simmer the gumbo for 50 to 60 minutes or until chicken is tender. Stir frequently being careful not to break the chicken pieces.

■ Remove pot from the heat, letting the simmer die. Add filé powder and stir. Let gumbo stand for 5 minutes after adding the filé. Serve in bowls over rice.

Good Lord, make us thankful for these and all our blessings. Pardon our sins and save us. Amen.

Hardy Family Blessing

Barley Soup

Ingram Pharmacy

Yield: 4 to 5 servings

1	medium onion, chopped	2	carrots, diced
2	cloves garlic, crushed	½	cup chopped celery
2	tablespoons olive oil	1	teaspoon salt
½	cup barley		Dash of red pepper flakes
1	cup chopped cooked chicken	2	quarts water
		¼	cup chopped parsley

■ Sauté onion and garlic in olive oil. Add barley, chicken, carrots, celery, salt, pepper and water. Bring to a boil and cover. Simmer until barley and vegetables are tender (about 45 minutes). Add parsley for final 5 minutes.

This recipe was on a napkin at Ingram's lunch counter.

Brunswick Stew

Yield: 15 servings

7	boneless, skinless chicken breasts	2	(10-ounce) packages frozen corn
	Water for cooking	¾	cup diced green pepper
3-4	tablespoons chicken bouillon	¾	cup chopped onion
2	(10-ounce) packages frozen lima beans	1	cup chopped celery
2	(10-ounce) packages frozen cut green beans	5-6	(14½-ounce) cans stewed tomatoes

■ Cook chicken in a large stockpot with water to which bouillon has been added. When done, remove chicken from water. Pour off all but 4 cups of the broth.

■ Cut the chicken breasts into bite-sized pieces and return to the pot. Add lima beans, green beans, corn, green pepper, onions, celery and stewed tomatoes. Cook until vegetables are tender.

Soups, Salads & Dressings

OLD FASHIONED BRUNSWICK STEW

Yield: 8 to 10 servings

2	pounds chicken	2	stalks celery, chopped
5	cups water	½	stick butter
1½	quarts tomatoes		Salt
4	cups lima beans		Black pepper
2	cups corn	¼	teaspoon ground red pepper
2	cups chopped potatoes	¼	teaspoon sugar
2	medium onions, chopped	1	teaspoon oregano

■ In a large stockpot stew or boil chicken in water for 1 to 1½ hours. Remove the chicken, cool and cut into bite-sized pieces. Return chicken to the pot.

■ Add tomatoes, lima beans, corn, potatoes, onions, celery, butter, salt, pepper, red pepper, sugar and oregano. Cook for 4 hours over low heat. Stir often.

KAY'S SHE CRAB SOUP

Yield: 4 servings

8	tablespoons butter	1	teaspoon finely grated lemon zest
2	tablespoons flour	½	teaspoon mace
2	cups milk	½	teaspoon white pepper
2	cups heavy cream	1	teaspoon salt
1	pint backfin crabmeat	3	tablespoons dry sherry
1½	teaspoons finely grated onion		Parsley

■ Melt butter in a heavy 4-quart stockpot over moderate heat and stir in flour. Add milk and cream slowly and bring to a boil, stirring constantly.

■ Add crabmeat, onion, lemon zest, mace, white pepper and salt. Reduce heat and simmer partially covered for 20 minutes.

■ Just before serving, stir in sherry. Garnish bowls of soup with parsley and serve.

*E*ASY *O*YSTER *S*TEW

LUCKY STAR

Yield: 1 to 2 servings

1	pint milk	1	pint oysters with liquid
½	cup heavy cream	½	teaspoon black pepper
¼	cup butter		Coarse salt
½	cup washed and thinly sliced leeks		

- Preheat soup tureen and soup bowls.

- Heat the milk, cream, butter and leeks in a 2-quart saucepan or pot until just under a boil. Remove from heat and keep warm.

- In another saucepan, simmer the oysters in their own liquid until edges just begin to curl. Stir heated oysters into cream mixture and reheat to just under a boil. Season to taste with pepper and salt. Serve with oyster crackers.

*E*ASTERN *S*HORE-*S*TYLE *C*LAM *C*HOWDER

Yield: 12 servings

¼	pound bacon, cut into ¼-inch pieces	2	cups white wine
1	medium yellow onion, peeled and diced	4	cups clam juice
4	stalks celery, diced	4	cups water
2	carrots, peeled and finely diced		Coarse salt to taste
4	medium white potatoes, diced		White pepper to taste
1	bunch parsley, washed and chopped	2	quarts large clams, well-rinsed and cut into medium-sized pieces
1	tablespoon fresh thyme		

- Fry bacon in a large stockpot over low heat. When bacon is crisp, add onions, celery and carrots and sauté until onions are just soft.

- Add potatoes, parsley and thyme. Pour in wine, clam juice and water. Cook until potatoes are soft. Season with salt and white pepper. Add clams and simmer until they are just done, about 4 to 5 minutes.

- Serve with crackers.

CHINESE CHICKEN SALAD

Yield: 4 to 6 servings

Salad

4	boneless, skinless chicken breast halves
2	medium cloves garlic, minced
2-3	tablespoons oil or butter
	Salt
	Pepper

1	head romaine or ½ head iceberg lettuce
1	(15-ounce) can pineapple chunks, drained
1	(8-ounce) can sliced water chestnuts, drained

Dressing

¼	cup safflower or vegetable oil
4-5	teaspoons white wine vinegar
4	tablespoons sugar
2-3	teaspoons salt

	Pepper to taste
1	cup slivered almonds
1-2	tablespoons sesame seeds

■ Cut chicken into finger-width strips. Sauté chicken with garlic in oil or butter. Add salt and pepper to taste.

■ Shred or tear lettuce and place in salad bowl. Add the pineapple, water chestnuts and cooked chicken.

■ For the dressing, combine the oil, vinegar, sugar, salt and pepper and whisk vigorously to incorporate sugar. Pour dressing over the chicken salad. Sprinkle with almonds and sesame seeds.

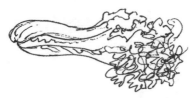

GARDEN TOUR LUNCHEON CHICKEN SALAD

Yield: 4 servings

1	pound boneless, skinless chicken breasts, cooked and chopped
1	cup seedless green grapes, halved
½	cup slivered almonds

4	tablespoons mayonnaise
1½	tablespoons mustard-mayonnaise sauce

■ Combine the chicken, grapes and almonds. Mix in mayonnaise and sauce. Coat well. Chill.

■ Serve on mixed salad greens.

Light Chicken Salad

Yield: 4 servings

Salad

1	cup cooked, diced chicken	1	green onion, chopped
12	cherry tomatoes, halved		Lettuce or spinach leaves
1	yellow pepper, seeded and chopped		

Dressing

2	tablespoons fresh lemon juice	¼	teaspoon pepper
1	tablespoon olive oil		Dash salt
¼	teaspoon dry mustard		

■ Combine the chicken, tomatoes, yellow pepper and onion in a bowl.

■ Whisk or blend the lemon juice, olive oil, mustard, pepper and salt. Drizzle over the salad. Refrigerate for several hours. Lightly toss and serve on a bed of lettuce or spinach leaves.

Curried Chicken Salad

Yield: 6 servings

2	teaspoons lime juice	1	Granny Smith apple, chopped
¾	teaspoon curry powder	¾	cup dried cranberries
¾	cup mayonnaise	½	cup diced celery
2	cups cooked, diced chicken	¼	cup pecan pieces

■ Stir the lime juice and curry powder into the mayonnaise and set aside.

■ Mix the chicken, apple, cranberries, celery and pecans in a large bowl. Add the curry mixture and mix well.

■ Chill and serve on a bed of lettuce.

ORZO AND CHICKEN SALAD

Yield: 4 servings

1 cup uncooked orzo pasta	1 (7¾-ounce) can chickpeas, drained
1 (3-ounce) package pre-grilled chicken pieces	⅓ cup pitted, coarsely chopped kalamata olives
1 (6-ounce) jar marinated artichoke hearts, drained and chopped	1 (4-ounce) package reduced-fat feta cheese, crumbled
1 cup grape or cherry tomatoes, halved	⅓ cup prepared vinaigrette salad dressing

- Cook orzo according to package directions. Rinse with cold water and drain well.

- Combine pasta, chicken, artichokes, tomatoes, chickpeas, olives and feta cheese.

- Toss with the vinaigrette. Chill at least 30 minutes before serving.

CHICKEN PINEAPPLE SALAD

Yield: 4 to 6 servings

Salad

4 cups cooked cubed chicken breast	½ cup halved seedless grapes
1½ cups thinly sliced celery	1 cup chopped water chestnuts
1 (8-ounce) can of pineapple tidbits, well-drained	½ cup chopped almonds

Dressing

1½ cups mayonnaise	½ teaspoon curry powder
1 tablespoon soy sauce	Juice of 1 lemon

- For dressing, combine mayonnaise, soy sauce, curry powder and lemon juice in a jar and refrigerate.

- Combine chicken, celery, pineapple, grapes, water chestnuts and almonds. Add dressing at serving time.

Chinese Chicken Salad

Thalhimer's

Yield: 6 servings

Dressing

3½	tablespoons soy sauce	½	teaspoon garlic powder
2	tablespoons vegetable oil	½	teaspoon pepper
2	tablespoons rice vinegar	½	teaspoon sesame oil
1	tablespoon sugar		

Salad

4	cups torn lettuce, divided	½	cup julienned carrots
1½	cups chopped cooked chicken	¼	cup diagonally sliced green onions
1	(8-ounce) can sliced water chestnuts, drained	¼	cup chopped red cabbage
		1	(5-ounce) can chow-mein noodles

■ For dressing, whisk soy sauce, vegetable oil, vinegar, sugar, garlic powder, pepper and sesame oil in a small bowl. Set aside.

■ In a large bowl combine 2 cups lettuce, chicken, water chestnuts, carrots, green onions and red cabbage.

■ Just before serving, toss with dressing and top with noodles. Serve on a bed of remainder of lettuce.

Shrimp, Artichoke and Couscous Salad

Yield: 6 servings

1½	pounds unpeeled fresh shrimp	¼	cup mayonnaise
½	cup uncooked couscous	⅓	cup juice of fresh lemon
½	red pepper, chopped	3	tablespoons chopped fresh dill
½	green pepper, chopped		Salt
1	(14-ounce) can artichoke hearts, drained and chopped		Pepper

■ Boil shrimp for 3 minutes or until pink. Rinse, peel and devein, then cut in half lengthwise. Chill.

■ Cook couscous according to package directions. Place in a large bowl to cool. Stir with a fork to fluff. Add the cooled shrimp, peppers and artichoke hearts and mix well.

■ Combine mayonnaise, lemon juice and fresh dill. Pour over salad and lightly toss.

■ Cover salad and chill at least 2 hours before serving.

Soups, Salads & Dressings

CURRIED RICE AND SHRIMP SALAD

Yield: 6 to 8 servings

1	pound large shrimp, shelled, deveined and cooked		Salt and pepper
1½	cups white rice	1	red apple, unskinned and chopped
3	tablespoons mayonnaise	2	slices fresh pineapple, cut into pieces
2	teaspoons curry powder	2	tablespoons raisins
1	tablespoon soy sauce	2	tablespoons peanuts
1	tablespoon Worcestershire sauce	¼	cup grated coconut plus garnish
¼	teaspoon dry mustard		Lettuce

- Prepare shrimp and chill.

- Cook and cool rice.

- Blend mayonnaise, curry powder, soy sauce, Worcestershire sauce and mustard. Season to taste with salt and pepper.

- Combine rice and curried mayonnaise mixture.

- Fold in shrimp, apple, pineapple, raisins, peanuts and coconut. Sprinkle additional coconut for garnish, if desired.

This recipe hails from Tortola, a tiny island in the British Virgin Islands. Serve with or without shrimp.

CRAB SALAD

Yield: 4 servings

1	pound lump crabmeat		Juice of 1 lemon
1	cup chopped celery		Mayonnaise
½	cup diced cucumber	3	hard-cooked eggs, quartered
¼	teaspoon salt		
Dash of black pepper			

- Combine the crabmeat, celery, cucumber, salt and pepper. Sprinkle lemon juice over the mixture and add just enough mayonnaise to moisten.

- Toss the salad gently and garnish with egg quarters. Chill.

Lump Crabmeat and Baked Asparagus Salad

Lucky Star

Yield: 6 servings

2	pounds asparagus, trimmed and peeled, if necessary	1	pound prosciutto, very thinly sliced
1	cup plus 1 tablespoon olive oil, divided	½	pound mesclun greens
		1	pound lump crabmeat
1	pinch coarse salt	½	cup lemon juice
1	pinch coarsely ground black pepper	¼	pound fresh Parmesan cheese, shaved

- Preheat oven to 425 degrees.

- Place prepared asparagus in an ovenproof pan. Drizzle with 1 tablespoon olive oil. Season with salt and pepper. Cover with foil and bake until asparagus is tender, about 15 minutes. Uncover and cool in refrigerator.

- Assemble salad by placing slices of prosciutto on plates. Lay asparagus on the prosciutto with greens next to the asparagus spears. Top the greens with portions of crabmeat.

- Whisk lemon juice and olive oil. Drizzle dressing over the salads and garnish with shaved Parmesan cheese.

Oriental Pasta Salad

Yield: 6 to 8 servings

⅔	cup soy sauce	⅓	cup chopped green onions
⅔	cup vegetable oil	1	(8-ounce) can sliced water chestnuts, drained
1	tablespoon spicy hot Chinese oil		
6	tablespoons vinegar	1	cup snow peas
4	tablespoons sugar	1	pound shrimp, cooked, peeled and deveined or chicken, cooked, cubed (optional)
½	cup sesame seeds		
1	pound linguini, cooked and drained		

- For dressing, combine soy sauce, oils, vinegar, sugar and sesame seeds.

- Combine in a large bowl the linguini, green onion, water chestnuts and snow peas. For an entrée, add shrimp or chicken.

- Lightly toss the salad with the dressing. May be served chilled or at room temperature.

Greek Pasta Salad

Yield: 8 to 10 servings

12	ounces bow tie pasta
1	(16-ounce) can medium pitted ripe olives, drained
4	ounces crumbled feta cheese with basil and sun-dried tomatoes
1	pint cherry tomatoes, halved
1	bunch green onions, chopped
	Greek vinaigrette dressing

■ Cook pasta al dente, drain and cool. Toss the pasta with the olives, feta cheese, tomatoes and green onion.

■ Pour desired amount of prepared dressing over the salad and mix.

Shrimp Aspic Mold

Yield: 8 servings

1	(3-ounce) package lemon gelatin
1	cup very hot water
1	(10¾-ounce) can condensed tomato soup
2	tablespoons red wine vinegar
1	tablespoon grated onion
1	tablespoon prepared horseradish
1	(4¼-ounce) can shrimp

■ Dissolve the lemon gelatin in the hot water. Stir in the tomato soup, vinegar, onion and horseradish. Chill until slightly thickened.

■ Pour half the mixture in the bottom of a mold and arrange a layer of shrimp in a pattern. Return to refrigerator and chill until firm. Add the remaining shrimp and pour remaining gelatin mixture over the top. Chill until firm.

"I am the true vine, and my Father is the gardener. He cuts off every branch in me that bears no fruit, while every branch that does bear fruit he prunes so that it will be even more fruitful... I am the vine, you are the branches."

John 15:1-2, and 5

LIME SALAD

Yield: 8 to 10 servings

2 (3-ounce) packages lime gelatin	Maraschino cherries, halved
2 cups hot water	1 cup pecan pieces
1 (15-ounce) can crushed pineapple, drained	8 ounces sour cream

- Dissolve the lime gelatin in hot water and place in refrigerator until it has begun to set. Remove from refrigerator and beat with an electric mixer until the mixture is foamy.

- Add the pineapple, cherries, pecans and sour cream. Pour the mixture into molds and chill.

MOTHER'S GOOD CRANBERRY SALAD

Yield: 6 to 8 servings

1 (3-ounce) package raspberry or strawberry gelatin	½ cup drained crushed pineapple
1 cup boiling water	1 (16-ounce) can whole cranberry sauce
Juice of ½ lemon	½ cup chopped walnuts
1 cup diced celery	

- Dissolve the gelatin in the boiling water. Add lemon juice, celery, pineapple, cranberry sauce and walnuts.

- Pour in a 3-cup ring mold. Chill.

Mom's Ribbon Congealed Salad

Yield: 20 to 30 servings

2	(15½-ounce) plus 1 (6-ounce) cans crushed pineapple	3	(3-ounce) packages lemon-flavored gelatin (yellow)
2	(6-ounce) packages cherry or raspberry gelatin (red)	1	(8-ounce) plus 1 (4-ounce) packages cream cheese, softened
6	cups ice, divided	2	(6-ounce) packages lime-flavored gelatin (green)
40	large marshmallows		

■ Drain pineapple thoroughly and reserve liquid. Spray a 15 x 10 x 1-inch glass baking dish with vegetable cooking spray.

■ Prepare red gelatin by dissolving both packages in 3 cups boiling water. Stir well for 1 to 2 minutes. Stir in 3 cups of ice, about 36 cubes. Pour into prepared dish and refrigerate until this layer is firm.

■ Heat the marshmallows in 1 cup of reserved pineapple juice until completely melted.

■ Prepare lemon gelatin by mixing the 3 packages gelatin with 4 cups boiling water. Do not add ice. Set aside to cool.

■ Blend softened cream cheese into the marshmallow mixture, mixing until smooth and creamy.

■ Combine the lemon gelatin and cream cheese mixture. Fold in thoroughly drained pineapple. Pour onto the firm red layer. Allow this lemon layer to set well in refrigerator before adding the top green layer.

■ Mix the packages of lime-flavored gelatin with 3 cups boiling water. Dissolve thoroughly and stir in 3 cups of ice. When slightly congealed pour over the firm lemon layer. Cover with plastic wrap. Refrigerate overnight or until each layer is completely congealed. As salad cools, watch for condensation on plastic wrap and replace it if necessary.

STRAWBERRY SPINACH SALAD

Yield: 12 servings

Salad

1	(6-ounce) package baby spinach	2	(11-ounce) cans Mandarin oranges, drained
1	pint strawberries, washed, capped and sliced	¼	cup chopped pecans or walnuts
⅔	cup chopped green onions		

Orange Honey Dressing

1¼	cups orange juice	2	tablespoons canola oil
¼	cup honey	2	teaspoons Dijon mustard

- Combine spinach, strawberries, green onions, oranges and nuts in a salad bowl.

- In a covered container or blender, mix orange juice, honey, canola oil and mustard. Shake or blend until well mixed. Chill the dressing and toss with the salad.

SPICY ASIAN SLAW

Yield: 4 servings

3	tablespoons rice vinegar	1	head cabbage, grated or 1 (8-ounce) package coleslaw mix
2	tablespoons soy sauce		
1	tablespoon sesame oil		
¼	teaspoon crushed red pepper flakes	½	cup raisins
		⅓	cup thinly sliced scallions
		¼	cup chopped peanuts or cashews

- In a large bowl whisk vinegar, soy sauce, sesame oil and crushed red pepper.

- Add grated cabbage or coleslaw mix, raisins and scallions to the dressing. Toss well. Chill at least 1 hour. Serve with chopped nuts sprinkled on top.

BROOK'S SALAD

Yield: 4 servings

1 avocado, chopped	2 cups shredded lettuce
2 tomatoes, chopped	1 heaping tablespoon mayonnaise
Green onions, chopped	Chili powder
2 cloves garlic, minced or pressed	Lemon pepper

- Combine avocado, tomatoes, onions, garlic and lettuce.

- Season mayonnaise to taste with chili powder and lemon pepper. Toss vegetables with mayonnaise mixture.

- Serve salad alone or on bed of lettuce.

SPINACH, APPLE AND BACON SALAD

Yield: 6 servings

Salad

1 pound fresh spinach, torn	3 green onions, chopped
1 red apple, unpeeled and coarsely chopped	¼ pound bacon, fried and crumbled

Mustard Dressing

¼ cup olive oil	1 tablespoon prepared mustard
3 tablespoons red wine vinegar	Salt
1 teaspoon sugar	Pepper

- Combine the spinach, apple and green onions in a salad bowl. Crumble the bacon over the salad.

- In a blender or other container, combine the oil, vinegar, sugar and mustard. Blend or shake well. Add desired amount of salt and pepper.

- Toss the salad with the dressing and serve.

Yummy Salad

Yield: 10 to 12 servings

Salad

1	pound fresh broccoli florets
1	pound fresh cauliflower florets
½	cup raisins

⅓	cup finely chopped red onion
6	slices bacon, cooked and crumbled

Sunflower Seed Dressing

1	cup mayonnaise
¼	cup sugar
2	tablespoons cider vinegar

Fresh ground pepper
½ cup sunflower kernels

- Toss the broccoli, cauliflower, raisins, onion and bacon in a large bowl.

- Combine the mayonnaise, sugar, vinegar and pepper. Add dressing to the salad and thoroughly mix. Refrigerate covered for at least 2 hours.

- Just before serving, add the sunflower kernels and toss.

Frozen Pea Salad

Yield: 8 to 10 servings

1	(10-ounce) package frozen peas, thawed
6	green onions, chopped
4-6	ounces salted cashews or sunflower seeds
2	cloves garlic, pressed

½ cup sour cream
¼ cup mayonnaise
Juice of 1 lemon
Lemon pepper
Salt

- Combine the thawed peas, green onions, cashews or sunflower seeds and garlic.

- Mix sour cream, mayonnaise and lemon juice. Pour over pea mixture and toss lightly to coat. Season to taste with lemon pepper and salt.

- Chill at least 6 hours before serving. Serve alone or in avocado halves or lettuce cups.

Great Layered Salad

Yield: 12 servings

1	pound fresh spinach, torn	1	(10-ounce) package frozen peas, thawed
1	medium head iceberg lettuce, torn	1	cup mayonnaise
6	eggs, hard-cooked and sliced	½	cup sour cream
1	pound bacon, cooked and crumbled	½	(4-ounce) package buttermilk-mayonnaise dressing mix
1	(8-ounce) can sliced water chestnuts, drained		Chopped fresh parsley (optional)

- In a large salad bowl layer the spinach, lettuce, eggs, bacon, water chestnuts and peas.

- In another container combine the mayonnaise, sour cream and dressing mix. Mix thoroughly. Spread over the layered vegetables and cover all the way to the edge of the salad bowl. Garnish with parsley and cover tightly. Refrigerate several hours or overnight.

Delicious Layered Pea Salad

Yield: 10 to 12 servings

1	head lettuce, torn into small pieces	1	(10-ounce) package frozen peas, separated but not thawed
1½	cups chopped celery	½	cup mayonnaise
½-¾	cup chopped green onion	8	slices bacon, fried and crumbled
½	cup chopped green pepper	2	cups shredded Cheddar cheese

- Place lettuce in the bottom of a large bowl. Layer the celery, green onion, green pepper and peas over the lettuce.

- Spread mayonnaise over top of the frozen peas. Spread all the way to the edge to seal.

- Sprinkle a layer of bacon over the mayonnaise. Top with a layer of cheese.

- Cover salad with plastic wrap and chill at least 6 hours before serving.

Tailgate Potato Salad

Yield: 4 servings

Vinaigrette Dressing

½ cup extra-virgin olive oil
¼ cup white wine vinegar

1 teaspoon salt
Freshly ground black pepper

Salad

1 cup green beans, trimmed and cut into 1-inch pieces
1 pound new red potatoes
¾ cup crumbled feta cheese
¾ cup sliced black olives

½ cup sliced green onions
¼ cup finely diced green pepper
¾ cup sliced radishes
Lettuce leaves

- For dressing, combine olive oil, vinegar, salt and black pepper. Whisk thoroughly. Set aside.

- Add the green beans to a saucepan of boiling water and cook about 4½ minutes. Drain, rinse beans in cold water and drain again.

- Place peeled or unpeeled potatoes in a pot of salted cold water. Bring to a boil and cook approximately 20 minutes until potatoes are tender, but firm. Drain and quarter potatoes and place them in a large bowl.

- Sprinkle the vinaigrette dressing over the potatoes and beans. Add feta cheese, olives, onions, pepper and radishes. Toss lightly to mix. Cool salad to room temperature. Cover and refrigerate overnight. Serve on a bed of lettuce leaves.

Red, White and Bleu Slaw

Yield: 6 to 8 servings

6 cups coarsely chopped green cabbage
½ cup bacon, cooked and crumbled

¾ cup crumbled bleu cheese, divided
1 cup prepared coleslaw dressing
Cherry tomatoes

- Combine the cabbage, bacon, ½ cup bleu cheese and slaw dressing. Mix well and chill.

- To serve, garnish with cherry tomatoes and remaining bleu cheese.

"Spanish Fisherman"
by Carol De Bolt Eikenberry

Entrées

Entrées

BAKED SPAGHETTI

Yield: 8 generous servings

1	pound spaghetti	1	(10¾-ounce) can cream of mushroom soup
1	pound lean ground beef		
1	onion, chopped	1½	cups water
1	green pepper, chopped	1	(10¾-ounce) can tomato soup
2	cloves garlic, chopped	3	cups shredded sharp Cheddar cheese, divided
1	(6-ounce) can pitted, sliced black olives, drained (optional)		
		1	(26-ounce) jar spaghetti sauce
			Grated Parmesan cheese

- Cook spaghetti in boiling water for 8 to 10 minutes or until al dente. Drain pasta and reserve.

- Preheat oven to 350 degrees. Grease a 9 x 13 x 2-inch baking dish.

- In a large skillet over medium heat, brown the beef and sauté the onion, green pepper and garlic. Pour off excess liquid and grease. Mix in black olives.

- In a medium-sized saucepan or bowl, combine the mushroom soup, water and tomato soup.

- Spread half the cooked pasta in the prepared baking dish. Spoon half the beef mixture over the spaghetti. Pour half the soup mixture over the beef and spread 1½ cups Cheddar cheese over it. Repeat layers of pasta, beef, soup and Cheddar cheese.

- Pour spaghetti sauce over all. Sprinkle Parmesan cheese on top. Bake until bubbly and lightly browned, 30 to 45 minutes.

STUFFED GREEN PEPPERS

Yield: 6 servings

Stuffed Peppers

6 large green peppers	⅔ cup uncooked white rice
2½ cups water, divided	1½ teaspoons salt
1 pound ground beef	⅛ teaspoon black pepper
2 tablespoons vegetable oil	¼ teaspoon garlic salt
1 medium onion, chopped	

Tomato Sauce

1 onion, sliced	Bouquet garni (peppercorns and cloves)
2 tablespoons butter	Salt
1 (10¾-ounce) can tomato soup	Black pepper
1 cup liquid reserved from boiling peppers	

- Preheat oven to 350 degrees.

- Remove tops and seeds from peppers, saving the tops. Parboil in 1½ cups water in a large covered pot for 5 minutes. Reserve the liquid and drain the peppers.

- In a large skillet brown ground beef in oil. Chop the pepper tops and stir with onion. Sauté for 5 minutes. Pour off excess grease.

- To prepare tomato sauce, sauté onion in butter in a medium-sized saucepan. Combine tomato soup, 1 cup pepper liquid and sautéed onion. Add bouquet garni and season to taste with salt and black pepper.

- Simmer the sauce for 5 minutes, stirring occasionally.

- Pour in rice, 1 cup tomato sauce and 1 cup water plus 1½ cups reserved liquid from the peppers. Season with salt, pepper and garlic salt. Simmer covered for 10 minutes until rice is half cooked and some of the liquid remains. If the mixture is too dry, add ½ cup water or tomato sauce.

- Add rice mixture to the beef.

- Stuff the peppers three-fourths full of beef and rice mixture. Place peppers in a baking dish and bake for 1 hour. Cover each pepper with tomato sauce. Baste occasionally with sauce. Remove bouquet garni from sauce before serving.

CABBAGE AND MEATBALLS

Yield: 6 servings

1	(28-ounce) can tomatoes	1	head cabbage, cut into wedges
1	(14-ounce) can tomato sauce	1	pound ground beef
½	cup apple cider vinegar	1	egg
¾	cup brown sugar	¼	cup uncooked rice
2	tablespoons lemon juice	¼	teaspoon salt
1½	cups water		

- Combine tomatoes, tomato sauce, vinegar, brown sugar, lemon juice and water in a stockpot. Bring to a boil and add cabbage wedges.

- Mix ground beef, egg, rice and salt. Roll into meatballs. Drop meatballs into the cabbage mixture. Turn heat down to low.

- Simmer 2 hours.

MEATLOAF

Yield: 6 servings

1	pound ground beef	¼	cup milk
½	pound ground sausage or ground turkey	1	(8-ounce) can tomato sauce, divided
2	onions, chopped	½	cup ketchup
1-2	cloves garlic, chopped	2	teaspoons salt
2	stalks celery, chopped with leaves	½	teaspoon pepper
1	egg	1½	cups breadcrumbs

- Preheat oven to 350 degrees. Grease a 9 x 5 x 2-inch loaf pan.

- Combine ground beef, sausage or turkey, onion, garlic and celery. Mix thoroughly. Combine and stir the egg, milk, half the tomato sauce, ketchup, salt and pepper and mix into the meat mixture. Mix in breadcrumbs.

- Form into a loaf and bake for 1 hour. Remove from the oven and pour the remaining tomato sauce over the top. Return to oven and bake another 15 minutes.

Hawaiian Shish-Kabob

Yield: 4 to 6 servings

1	pound round steak, lamb or boneless chicken	1	clove garlic, cut
1	cup pineapple juice (from canned pineapple chunks)	4	firm tomatoes
		2	large Vidalia onions
½	cup soy sauce	2	green peppers
1	tablespoon ground ginger	1	(16-ounce) can pineapple chunks

■ Preheat oven to broil.

■ Cut meat into cubes. Combine pineapple juice, soy sauce, ginger and garlic. Marinate beef cubes for several hours or overnight.

■ Cut tomatoes and onions into wedges. Cut peppers into pieces.

■ Place meat, tomatoes, onion, green pepper and pineapple chunks on skewers, alternating meat, vegetable and fruit; begin and end with meat.

■ Broil kabobs, turning once. Baste with marinade once or twice and watch vegetables closely. Slide off skewers and serve with rice.

Beef Tenderloin

Yield: 8 to 12 servings

Beef Tenderloin

2	tablespoons seasoned salt	1	teaspoon salt
1	tablespoon fresh ground black pepper	1	tablespoon soy sauce
		4-5	pound beef tenderloin, trimmed of fat

Sauce

1	(5-ounce) jar prepared horseradish	½	teaspoon Worcestershire sauce
1	cup French onion dip	1	tablespoon hot pepper sauce

■ Preheat broiler.

■ Combine seasoned salt, pepper, salt and soy sauce. Rub into trimmed tenderloin, coating both sides.

■ Broil meat for 7½ minutes on each side. Turn oven to 350 degrees. Cover tenderloin with foil and bake for 35 minutes or to desired doneness.

■ Mix horseradish, onion dip, Worcestershire sauce and hot pepper sauce. Serve with beef tenderloin.

*P*olly Altizer's mother-in-law, Anna Mae Wilkinson, is a graduate of Skidmore College. This recipe is from the Skidmore Alumnae Recipes.

GRILLED LUCAS LAMB CHOPS

Yield: 6 servings

6	(1½-inch thick) lamb chops, trimmed		Coarse salt
¼	cup mint sauce or mint jelly, divided		Coarse black pepper
¾	cup red port	3	teaspoons minced garlic

- Place chops in a covered container so that each chop can lie flat. Pierce each chop liberally with a fork.
- Combine half the mint sauce with the red port. Pour over the chops. Season liberally with salt and pepper, rubbing it into the meat with the back of a fork.
- Place ⅛ to ¼ teaspoon garlic on each chop followed by ¼ teaspoon of mint sauce. Turn chops and repeat on the other side.
- Cover and marinate for at least 4 hours.
- Preheat grill on high for 4 minutes.
- Place chops on hot grill and sear on each side for approximately 30 seconds. Turn grill down to medium heat and cook chops for 5 minutes on each side. Watch chops to control flame flare-ups.

Jacquelyn Lucas likes the chops to be almost rare so that when the meat is done it should feel like the center of your palm when pressed down.

BARBECUED LEG OF LAMB

Yield: Depends on size of leg of lamb

1	leg of lamb	1	cup vinegar
1	large onion, sliced	1	cup ketchup
1	cup water	1	tablespoon Worcestershire sauce
2	tablespoons dry mustard	½	teaspoon hot pepper sauce
1	tablespoon salt	2	tablespoons sugar
2	cloves garlic, slivered		

- Preheat oven to 325 degrees.
- Place leg of lamb and onion in a roasting pan. Pour 1 cup water in bottom of pan. Mix the mustard and salt and rub into lamb. Make small slits in the lamb and place garlic slivers in them.
- Bake covered for 45 minutes. Baste meat with all the vinegar. Continue cooking for about 2¼ hours more.
- Combine ketchup, Worcestershire sauce, hot pepper sauce and sugar and mix well.
- Spoon barbecue sauce over lamb 25 minutes before done. Continue cooking until total cooking time is 3 hours or meat thermometer registers desired doneness.

GRILLED ROSEMARY LAMB CHOPS

Yield: 6 servings

6 (1-inch thick) lamb chops, trimmed	½ teaspoon coarsely ground black pepper
¾ cup dry red wine	¼ teaspoon salt
3 tablespoons chopped fresh rosemary, divided	1 tablespoon butter
2 teaspoons minced garlic	Fresh rosemary sprigs
1 tablespoon balsamic vinegar	

■ Place chops in a roasting bag and set in a shallow dish.

■ Add the red wine, 2 tablespoons chopped rosemary, minced garlic, balsamic vinegar, pepper and salt to the roasting bag. Seal the bag and marinate chops in the refrigerator at least 2 hours and as long as 48 hours. Turn the bag occasionally while chops marinate.

■ Remove the chops from marinade and drain well. Reserve the marinade.

■ Prepare the grill. Cook chops on the grate of an uncovered grill directly over medium hot coals to desired doneness, 12 to 14 minutes for medium rare or 15 to 17 minutes for medium. Turn chops once during grilling and season to taste with salt and pepper.

■ While chops cook, strain the marinade into a small saucepan. Simmer, uncovered, over medium heat for about 5 minutes or until it is reduced to ⅓ cup. Stir in butter and remaining chopped rosemary and cook for 1 minute.

■ Serve chops with the sauce and top with rosemary sprigs.

CASSOULET

Yield: 8 to 10 servings

2	pounds Italian sausage	2	green peppers, seeded and chopped
1	pound Polish sausage		
4	chicken breasts, boned and skinned	2	(15-ounce) cans white beans, drained
Olive oil for browning		1	teaspoon dried basil
1	large onion, sliced	1	teaspoon paprika
2	large cloves garlic, minced	¼	cup chopped parsley
		2	beef bouillon cubes
		1	cup water

■ Preheat oven to 350 degrees.

■ Brown sausages, cut into thirds and place in a large casserole dish. Brown chicken in small amount of olive oil and cut into bite-sized pieces. Place in casserole dish.

■ Sauté onion and garlic in remaining oil. Add green pepper and cook for 1 minute. Put onion, garlic and green peppers into dish with sausage. Add beans, basil, paprika and parsley and mix. Dissolve bouillon cubes in water. Pour over the meat and beans.

■ Cover and bake for 1 hour 15 minutes.

Basil

Stromboli

Yield: 6 servings

2	frozen bread dough loaves (each makes 3 strombolis)	4	tablespoons canola oil
2	teaspoons oregano		Shredded mozzarella and Cheddar cheese
2	teaspoons parsley		Pepperoni slices
2	teaspoons garlic powder		Toppings such as mushrooms, peppers, onions, and sausage
4	teaspoons grated Parmesan cheese		Marinara sauce
2	eggs, separated		

■ Preheat oven to 375 degrees.

■ Thaw and roll each loaf of bread dough into thin, long strips.

■ In a small bowl, mix the oregano, parsley, garlic powder, Parmesan cheese, egg yolks and oil into a paste. Spread paste on dough with fingers. Sprinkle shredded cheeses liberally on top of paste. Place pepperoni and other desired toppings on the cheese.

■ Cut each dough loaf into 3 sections. Roll dough like a jellyroll, pinching closed any open edges. Place on ungreased baking sheet.

■ Brush the strombolis with egg whites. Bake for 15 to 20 minutes or until golden brown.

■ Warm up marinara sauce and serve as a dipping sauce.

_S_AUSAGE _C_ASSEROLE

Yield: 8 to 10 servings

1	pound ground sausage	1	(3-ounce) can mushrooms
½	cup chopped onion	½	teaspoon salt
½	clove garlic, minced	⅛	teaspoon pepper
2	tablespoons cooking oil	1	(7-ounce) package macaroni, cooked
1	(8-ounce) can tomato sauce	2	cups shredded sharp Cheddar cheese
1	(6-ounce) can tomato paste		

■ Preheat oven to 350 degrees. Grease a 13 x 9 x 3-inch baking dish.

■ Sauté sausage, onion and garlic in oil until onion is golden. Pour in tomato sauce, tomato paste and mushrooms. Season with salt and pepper. Simmer for 15 minutes.

■ Mix the cooked macaroni and shredded cheese into the sausage. Pour into prepared baking dish.

■ Bake for 40 minutes. Serve with tossed salad and garlic bread.

_P_ORK _T_ENDERLOIN

Yield: 4 to 6 servings

2	(1-pound) pork tenderloins	2	cloves garlic, minced
¼	cup olive oil	1	teaspoon salt
1	tablespoon balsamic vinegar	2	shakes ground pepper
1	tablespoon chopped rosemary		

■ Preheat oven to 375 degrees.

■ Place tenderloins in a large plastic bag.

■ Combine oil, vinegar, rosemary, garlic, salt and pepper in a large measuring cup and pour into bag with tenderloin. Close bag and marinate for 1 hour.

■ Bake in marinade for 30 minutes.

■ Ladle marinade over sliced pork.

Pork Ville DuBois

Yield: 8 servings

1	(3 to 4-pound) boneless pork roast	2	Granny Smith apples, sliced ¼-inch thick
½	teaspoon dry mustard	2	red onions, sliced ¼-inch thick
1½	teaspoons ground ginger	2	tablespoons soy sauce
1	teaspoon thyme	½	cup sherry
½	teaspoon garlic powder	12	ounces orange marmalade

■ Slice the roast vertically into ¾-inch slices, cutting almost to the bottom. Sprinkle mustard, ginger, thyme and garlic powder over the roast.

■ Place a slice of apple and a slice of onion in each slit.

■ Combine the soy sauce, sherry and marmalade. Spoon mixture over the roast. Cover the roast tightly and marinate overnight in the refrigerator.

■ Preheat oven to 350 degrees.

■ Bring roast to room temperature. Cook, covered in foil, for 1 hour. Uncover and continue to cook for 15 minutes more. Place roast on a serving platter.

■ Place roasting pan on burner and thicken sauce, adding extra soy sauce, sherry and marmalade, if necessary. Serve sauce over the roast.

Pork Chop-Apple Casserole

Yield: 6 servings

6	pork chops	1	tablespoon brown sugar
Salt		Pinch nutmeg	
Black pepper		Pinch thyme	
½	cup seedless raisins, parboiled	Pinch mace	
		Pinch ground cloves	
5	tart apples, peeled and quartered	1	cup consommé
		1	tablespoon flour
12	small white onions	1	tablespoon currant jelly

- Preheat oven to 350 degrees.

- Trim fat from each chop and place the fat in a heavy skillet to melt. Heat and brown the chops in this fat.

- Season chops with salt and pepper. Place in a 13 x 9 x 3-inch baking dish. Surround chops with raisins, apples and onions. Sprinkle with brown sugar, nutmeg, thyme, mace and cloves. Pour consommé over all.

- Bake for 1¼ hours.

- Before serving pour liquid into a saucepan. Bring it to a boil and thicken with flour. Stir in jelly. Serve this sauce separately.

If your enemy is hungry feed him; if he is thirsty, give him something to drink.

Romans 12:20

Costolette Di Vitello alla Capricciosa

Il Giardino

Yield: 4 servings

Veal

1 large egg, beaten	4 (10-ounce) bone-in veal chops, pounded to ¼-inch thick
1 tablespoon grated Parmigiana cheese	1 cup flour
1 tablespoon chopped fresh parsley	1 cup plain breadcrumbs
Pinch salt	½ cup olive oil
Pinch pepper	

Tomato Salad Topping

3 Roma tomatoes, each cored and cut into 6 slices	¼ cup extra-virgin olive oil
½ medium onion, julienned	6 fresh basil leaves, torn
	Juice of ½ lemon
	Salt and pepper to taste

■ Combine eggs, Parmigiana cheese, parsley, salt and pepper.

■ Dredge veal chops in flour, dip in egg mixture and cover with breadcrumbs.

■ Pour olive oil in skillet and fry veal 3 minutes on each side over medium heat, until golden brown. Remove from pan and blot on paper towel to absorb excess oil.

■ In a stainless steel or ceramic bowl, toss tomatoes with onion, olive oil, basil, lemon juice, salt and pepper. Serve on top of chops.

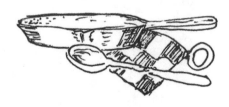

VEAL PARMIGIANA

Yield: 4 servings

2　tablespoons butter
4　(½-inch) veal cutlets, steaks or chops
⅔　cup evaporated milk, divided
½　cup plus 2 tablespoons grated
　　Parmesan cheese, divided

¼　cup all-purpose flour
½　teaspoon salt
Pinch pepper
1　(8-ounce) can tomato sauce

- Preheat oven to 350.

- Melt butter in an 8 x 12-inch pan. Dip veal into ⅓ cup milk and roll in 2 tablespoons Parmesan cheese mixed with flour, salt and pepper to coat. Bake uncovered for 30 minutes.

- Remove veal from the oven and pour tomato sauce over it. Mix rest of the milk with ½ cup cheese. Spoon mixture over the veal.

- Bake 20-35 minutes more until veal is tender.

VEAL CUTLET PARMESAN

Yield: 8 servings

1½　pounds (½-inch) veal cutlet, cut into
　　serving pieces
Salt
Pepper
1　cup saltine cracker crumbs
1　tablespoon minced parsley

1　clove garlic, minced
1½　tablespoons grated Parmesan
　　cheese
2　eggs
Olive oil

- Sprinkle cutlets with salt and pepper.

- Roll crackers in a plastic bag with a rolling pin. Mix cracker crumbs with parsley, garlic and cheese. Coat cutlets with crumb mixture, then dip in slightly beaten egg and then again in the crumbs. Pat crumbs firmly into the meat.

- Brown meat slowly in hot oil. Reduce heat and cook until tender.

Route 66 Lemon Pepper Chicken

Purple Cow Restaurant

Yield: 12 servings

When (Jesus) had finished speaking, he said to Simon, "Put out into deep water and let down the nets for a catch."

Luke 5:4

Chicken

12	portions cooked rice
¼	cup olive oil
1	cup finely diced onion
2	bay leaves
½	tablespoon chopped garlic

12 (6-ounce) boneless, skinless chicken breasts, cut into strips

Lemon pepper

1½ pounds fresh mushrooms, sliced

Lemon Pepper Gravy

2	quarts milk
1	(8-ounce) package white sauce mix
½	cup heavy cream
1	tablespoon chicken base

½ tablespoon ground white pepper

¼ cup lemon juice

Chopped parsley, tomato wedges and lemon slices for garnish

■ Cook rice and set aside. Keep rice hot.

■ Heat oil in a sauté pan and sauté onion, bay leaves and garlic.

■ Season chicken strips with lemon pepper. Sauté chicken and mushrooms in the onion mixture for several minutes. Stir and cover for 2 minutes.

■ For lemon pepper gravy, in a large pot whisk the cold milk with the white sauce mix until dissolved. Add cream, chicken base and white pepper. Cook gravy over low heat for 10 minutes, stirring often. Remove from heat and add lemon juice.

■ Place hot rice on plates, making a "nest" in the center. Spoon chicken mixture onto the rice and ladle hot gravy over the chicken. Garnish with parsley, tomato and lemon.

PAN-SEARED BALSAMIC CHICKEN

CYPRESS POINT COUNTRY CLUB

Yield: 4 servings

1	pound uncooked angel hair pasta	3-4	ounces balsamic vinegar
1	red pepper	1	clove garlic, minced
4	boneless, skinless chicken breasts	1	(10-ounce) bag fresh spinach, washed and stemmed
Salt		3-4	ounces white wine
Black pepper		4	ounces shredded Parmesan cheese
Olive oil, as needed			

- Preheat oven to 350 degrees.

- Cook and drain pasta. Set aside.

- Roast red pepper over an open flame. Peel off blackened skin and seed and julienne the pepper.

- Wash and pat the chicken dry. Season to taste with salt and pepper. Cover bottom of a heavy skillet with olive oil and heat until very hot. Sear chicken on both sides. Pour in vinegar and allow it to reduce while turning and stirring the chicken in the vinegar. The outer layer of the chicken should absorb the vinegar and turn brownish. The vinegar will scorch easily; take care not to burn it. Remove chicken to an ovenproof baking dish.

- Place garlic, roasted pepper, spinach and wine in pan with vinegar. Cook until spinach wilts. Top each chicken breast with an equal amount of spinach mixture. Sprinkle with Parmesan cheese. Finish cooking in the oven until chicken is done and cheese has melted and browned.

- Place chicken breasts on pasta. Drizzle pan drippings on top and serve with asparagus spears.

Then God said, "I give you every seed-bearing plant on the face of the whole earth, and every tree that has fruit with seed in it. They shall be yours for food."

Genesis 1:29

CHICKEN WITH ARTICHOKES

Yield: 6 servings

1½ cups sour cream (non-fat or light can be used)
1 teaspoon Worcestershire sauce
½ teaspoon hot pepper sauce
1 teaspoon salt
½ teaspoon white pepper
¼ teaspoon paprika

1 small garlic clove, minced
Juice of half a lemon
6 boneless, skinless chicken breasts
1 cup stale breadcrumbs
1 cup artichoke hearts, quartered
½ cup minced chives

- Preheat oven to 350 degrees. Grease a shallow baking dish.

- Mix sour cream, Worcestershire sauce, hot pepper sauce, salt, pepper, paprika, garlic and lemon juice.

- Dip chicken breasts in sour cream mixture and then in breadcrumbs. Place in prepared baking dish. Cover with foil and bake for one hour.

- Remove foil and sprinkle with artichoke hearts and chives. Uncover and bake for 15 minutes longer. Serve with rice.

ELAINE'S CHICKEN MARSALA

Yield: 4 servings

1 egg, beaten
3 tablespoons milk
1 pound of chicken breast, thinly sliced
2 tablespoons butter
1 clove garlic, minced

¾ cup water
1 cube chicken bouillon
2 tablespoons all-purpose flour
½ cup Marsala wine
¼ cup minced parsley
1 cup sliced mushrooms

- Mix egg and milk. Dip chicken in mixture and then into breadcrumbs spread in thin layer on a plate.

- Melt butter in frying pan and stir in the garlic. Fry chicken on both sides until lightly brown. Remove from pan and set aside.

- Mix water and bouillon and microwave until warm. Pour half the mixture into a pan with flour and stir until thick to make sauce. Reduce heat and stir in Marsala wine, parsley and mushrooms.

- Place chicken on heated serving platter. Pour Marsala sauce over chicken. Serve over cooked rice or pasta.

Chicken Supreme

Yield: 4 to 6 servings

⅓	cup all-purpose flour	¼	teaspoon thyme
¼	teaspoon salt	⅛	teaspoon garlic powder
⅛	teaspoon pepper	1	cup water
4-6	chicken breasts	¼	cup dry sherry
3	tablespoons butter	1	tablespoon lemon juice
1	(10-ounce) package onion soup mix		

- Preheat oven to 350 degrees.

- Combine flour, salt and pepper. Roll chicken in flour mixture and brown in pan with butter.

- Combine the onion soup mix, thyme, garlic powder, water, sherry and lemon juice. Pour over chicken in a large baking dish.

- Cover chicken and bake 45 minutes. Uncover and bake 15 minutes more.

Cornish Hens

Yield: 6 servings

6	Cornish hens, whole or split	2	tablespoons sherry or dry white wine
½	cup butter or margarine, melted		Juice of 1 lemon
1½	tablespoons cornstarch		Grated rind of 1 orange
1	cup orange juice	2	ounces current jelly or chutney
½	teaspoon thyme		

- Soak hens in salt water for 30 to 60 minutes. Drain and pat dry. Place hens in a 13 x 9 x 3-inch baking dish.

- Preheat oven to 325 degrees.

- Make sauce by combining the butter, cornstarch, orange juice, thyme, sherry or wine, lemon juice, orange rind and jelly. Pour over the hens.

- Bake for 60 minutes, basting frequently.

A whole roaster may be used instead of Cornish hens. Adjust the cooking time accordingly.

Sweet Bourbon Street Chicken

Yield: 6 to 8 servings

2	tablespoons teriyaki sauce	1	cup white grape juice, divided
½	teaspoon Worcestershire sauce	1½	pounds chicken, cut in bite-sized
½	teaspoon garlic salt		pieces
½	teaspoon ground ginger	¼	cup water, if needed
3	tablespoons brown sugar, divided	2	tablespoons sugar

- Mix the teriyaki sauce, Worcestershire sauce, garlic salt, ginger, 2 tablespoons brown sugar and ½ cup grape juice. Stir well.

- Pour ⅓ of the mixture over the chicken pieces. Toss until all are coated. Refrigerate overnight, if possible, but at least 3 hours. Save the remaining sauce and refrigerate separately.

- Simmer the marinated chicken, covered over medium-low heat until done. Remove chicken from the pan. Add the remaining brown sugar, grape juice, and water as needed to the pan. Bring to a simmer and stir until the sugar dissolves and sauce begins to thicken.

- Add chicken to the sauce, stirring until it is well coated and hot. Serve over rice.

Chick Jordan's Garlic Chicken Florentine

Yield: 6 servings

1	pound penne pasta	Dash white pepper	
3	pounds boneless, skinless chicken	1	red pepper, diced
	breasts	3	tablespoons prepared garlic
Olive oil		½	pound fresh spinach
Dash cardamom		1-2	cups heavy cream
Dash coriander		8	ounces grated Parmesan cheese

- Cook pasta according to package directions. Drain, cool and set aside.

- Cut chicken into strips. Sauté in olive oil with cardamom, coriander and white pepper. Set chicken aside.

- Sauté red pepper and garlic in olive oil. Stir in spinach. As spinach wilts, stir in sautéed chicken and 1 cup cream mixed with Parmesan cheese.

- Cook until cream is reduced. Toss with pasta and serve. For thicker sauce, add Parmesan; for thinner sauce add additional cream.

Mexican Chicken Lasagna

Yield: 10 to 12 servings

Chicken

4-6 chicken breast halves, cooked and diced to equal 4 cups

2 cups sour cream

1 cup diced green chili peppers or ½ cup canned, drained

1 (3½-ounce) can sliced ripe olives, drained

½-1 tablespoon jalapeño pepper, chopped (optional)

1 pound Cheddar cheese, shredded and divided

1 pound Monterey Jack cheese, shredded and divided

1 (11½-ounce) package flour tortillas (7½ inches)

Enchilada Sauce

2 tablespoons oil

½ cup onion, chopped

4 cloves garlic, peeled and crushed

2 cups tomatoes, chopped

1 (15-ounce) can tomato sauce

1 cup chicken broth

½ teaspoon salt

1 teaspoon cumin

1½ teaspoons chili powder

- Preheat oven to 375 degrees. Grease a 13 x 9 x 3-inch baking dish.

- Mix diced chicken, sour cream, green chili peppers, black olives, jalapeño pepper and all but 4 ounces of each of the cheeses. Reserved cheese will be used to top the casserole. Set aside.

- To make enchilada sauce, place oil in a medium saucepan and cook onion and garlic for 2 to 3 minutes on medium heat. Add tomatoes, tomato sauce, chicken broth, salt, cumin and chili powder. Simmer for 5 to 10 minutes.

- To assemble, place 1 cup of enchilada sauce in baking dish. Coat each side of eight tortillas with just enough enchilada sauce to moisten them. Lay two and one-half tortillas on sauce in dish. Layer one-third chicken mixture over tortillas and repeat each step, softening each tortilla in sauce before layering, until the filling is gone. Place a last layer of tortilla on top. Pour remaining enchilada sauce on top. (The dish can be covered and stored in refrigerator for up to 1 day, if desired.) Bake for 35 to 40 minutes. Top with the remaining cheese for the last 5 minutes of cooking.

Cilantro

Baked Chicken Breasts

Yield: 6 servings

2	cups sour cream	3	teaspoons salt
¼	cup fresh lemon juice	¼	teaspoon pepper
2	teaspoons Worcestershire sauce	6	boneless, skinless chicken breasts
1	teaspoon celery salt	1¾	cups stuffing mix, finely crumbled
1½	teaspoons paprika		

- Combine the sour cream, lemon juice, Worcestershire sauce, celery salt, paprika, salt and pepper.
- Wipe chicken breasts dry and place them into the sour cream mixture, coating each piece. Cover the chicken in the sour cream and refrigerate overnight.
- Preheat oven to 350 degrees. Remove chicken from the sour cream. Roll each piece in the stuffing mix.
- Bake uncovered for 45 minutes to 1 hour.

This recipe may be served at room temperature.

Alba's Chicken Enchiladas

Yield: 6 to 8 servings

4-6	boneless, skinless chicken breasts	1	(16-ounce) package shredded Cheddar cheese, divided
½	teaspoon olive oil		
1	(26-ounce) jar of pasta sauce	1	(6-ounce) can chopped ripe olives, drained and divided
½	cup taco sauce		
1	cup water	1	(14-ounce) package flour tortillas

- Preheat oven to 350 degrees.
- Cook chicken in hot olive oil until done. Dice the cooked chicken.
- In a saucepan, combine pasta sauce, taco sauce and water. Stir in chicken and ½ the cheese. Cook over medium heat until cheese is melted.
- Heat tortillas in microwave for 30 seconds to soften them.
- Fill each tortilla with a spoonful of the chicken mixture. Top mixture with a little more cheese and ripe olives. Fold tortilla and place in a 13 x 9 x 3-inch baking dish. Spread the remaining sauce over the folded tortillas and top with the remaining cheese.
- Bake for 20 minutes.

Mexican Chicken Casserole

Yield: 8 to 10 servings

1 large onion, chopped	1 (10½-ounce) can enchilada sauce (mild or hot)
Butter or margarine	
1 (8-ounce) can chopped chili peppers, drained	1 (10¾-ounce) can cream of chicken soup
1 (14 ounce) package flour tortillas	1 (5-ounce) can evaporated milk or 1 cup whole milk
4 cups cooked boned and diced chicken	2 cups chicken broth
2 cups shredded Cheddar cheese	

- Sauté onion in a small amount of butter or margarine. Stir in chili peppers and set aside.

- Line a 3-quart baking dish with approximately 5 uncooked tortillas. Next, spread layers of chicken, then cheese, sautéed onions and chili peppers, and broken tortilla pieces. Repeat the layers, ending with a topping of cheese.

- Thoroughly blend the soup, milk, broth and enchilada sauce. Pour over the casserole and refrigerate, covered, overnight.

- Preheat oven to 350 degrees and allow casserole to reach room temperature. Bake for 1 hour.

This recipe may be baked immediately for ½ hour.

He turned the desert into pools of water and the parched ground into flowing springs; there he brought the hungry to live, and they founded a city where they could settle. They sowed fields and planted vineyards that yielded a fruitful harvest; he blessed them, and their numbers greatly increased, and he did not let their herds diminish.

Psalm 107:35-38

Caddye's Chicken and Dumplings

Yield: 8 to 10 servings

Chicken

1 (5-pound) chicken	2 chicken bouillon cubes

Dumplings

2½ cups all-purpose flour	¾ cup water
¾ tablespoon salt	Salt
¾ stick butter	Pepper
1 egg	

■ Boil chicken, remove from water and pick meat from the bones. Remove the fat from the remaining chicken broth by refrigerating it or skimming. Add bouillon cubes to remaining liquid.

■ For dumplings, mix the flour and salt. Blend in butter by hand, like pie crust. When mixture is thoroughly blended make a hole or well in the center of the flour mixture. Break an egg into the well and pour water over the egg. Blend egg and water into the mixture by hand. Roll dough on a floured surface, seasoning to taste with salt and pepper. Slice dough into thin strips.

■ Bring stock to a boil.

■ Drop dough strips into boiling stock with the picked chicken meat. Cook for 10 minutes on medium boil. Turn off heat and leave covered pot on the burner for 30 minutes before serving.

HONEY-PECAN CRUSTED CHICKEN

Yield: 8 servings

¼	teaspoon salt	2	tablespoons Dijon mustard
¼	teaspoon pepper	¾	teaspoon paprika
4	(6-ounce) chicken breast halves, skinned	⅛	teaspoon garlic powder
8	(4-ounce) chicken drumsticks, skinned	1¼	cups finely crushed corn flakes cereal
¼	cup honey	½	cup finely chopped pecans

- Preheat oven to 400 degrees. Spray a 15 x 10-inch baking sheet with cooking spray.
- Sprinkle salt and pepper over chicken evenly. Set aside.
- Combine honey, mustard, paprika and garlic powder in a small bowl. Mix thoroughly.
- In a shallow dish, mix the corn flakes and pecans.
- Brush both sides of the chicken pieces with the honey mixture. Dredge each piece with pecan mixture and place on prepared baking sheet.
- Bake for 40 minutes.

VIRGINIA BEACH CHICKEN

Yield: 4 servings

⅓	pound bacon, fried	1	cup sour cream
4	chicken breast halves	½	cup burgundy, rosé or dry white wine
1	(10¾-ounce) can cream of mushroom soup		

- Preheat oven to 350 degrees.
- Remove cooked bacon from pan and crumble it. Pour off most of the bacon grease. Brown the chicken breasts in remaining bacon grease.
- Blend the mushroom soup, sour cream and wine. Place browned chicken in a 13 x 9 x 3-inch baking dish. Pour wine sauce over chicken and sprinkle bacon bits over top.
- Bake for 45 minutes to 1 hour. Serve over wild rice.

Chicken Barbecue

Yield: 5 servings

¼	pint vegetable oil	1½	teaspoons poultry seasoning
½	pint cider vinegar		
5	teaspoons salt	1	egg, well beaten
¼	teaspoon pepper	2½-3	pounds chicken

- Combine the oil, vinegar, salt, pepper, poultry seasoning and egg and mix well.
- Seal in plastic bag with chicken for at least 1 hour.
- Baste and turn chicken often while grilling.

Myrnie Howard suggests partially cooking poultry before grilling.

Swiss Chicken Casserole

Yield: 8 servings

8	boneless, skinless chicken breasts pounded flat	2-3	ounces water or dry sherry
1	(8-ounce) package sliced Swiss cheese	2	cups herb stuffing mix
		1	stick butter
1	(10¾-ounce) can cream of chicken or mushroom soup		

- Preheat oven to 350 degrees. Grease a 13 x 9 x 3-inch baking dish.
- Lay chicken breasts on the bottom of the prepared baking dish. Place Swiss cheese slices on top of chicken.
- Combine the soup and water or sherry and pour over cheese slices.
- Sprinkle stuffing mix over all and dot with butter.
- Bake covered for 30 minutes. Uncover and continue baking another 30 minutes.

CHICKEN POPPY SEED CASSEROLE

Yield: 8 to 12 servings

Casserole

4	chicken breasts	1	can water chestnuts, drained and sliced
1	cup sour cream		
1	(10¾-ounce) can cream of mushroom soup	1	tablespoon pimento
		1	teaspoon rosemary
1	(10¾-ounce) can cream of celery soup	1	tablespoon lemon juice
			Salt and pepper to taste
½	cup sliced almonds		

Topping

2	cups cracker crumbs	2	tablespoons poppy seeds
2	tablespoons grated Parmesan cheese	1	stick butter, melted

- Preheat oven to 350 degrees. Lightly grease a 13 x 9-inch baking dish.

- Cook chicken and cut into bite-size pieces. Mix chicken, sour cream, mushroom and celery soups, sliced almonds, water chestnuts, pimento, rosemary, lemon juice and salt and pepper. Spoon into prepared baking dish.

- Mix cracker crumbs, Parmesan cheese, poppy seeds and melted butter. Spread evenly over top of casserole. Bake for 30 minutes.

He makes the grass to grow for the cattle, and plants for man to cultivate— bringing forth food from the earth; wine that gladdens the heart of man, oil to make his face shine, and bread that sustains his heart.

Psalm 104:14

CHICKEN HAWAIIAN

Yield: 6 servings

Chicken

3 large boneless chicken breasts	¼ cup olive oil
1½ teaspoons salt	3 small pineapples
½ teaspoon pepper	2 (6-ounce) packages herb-seasoned rice

Sauce

2 tablespoons cornstarch	¾ cup firmly packed brown sugar
¾ cup water	¼ cup pineapple juice
¾ cup cider vinegar	¼ cup molasses

- Wash chicken breasts and pat dry. Cut each breast in half lengthwise. Sprinkle with salt and pepper. Sauté chicken in olive oil until brown on both sides. Remove chicken and set aside. Drain skillet.

- In same skillet, blend cornstarch with water until smooth. Stir in vinegar, brown sugar, pineapple juice and molasses. Cook on medium heat, stirring constantly, until sauce thickens and comes to a boil.

- Return chicken breasts to skillet, reduce heat and simmer in sauce, covered, 15 to 20 minutes until tender.

- Cut each pineapple in half lengthwise, cutting through frond. Cut out pineapple from each pineapple half, leaving a ½-inch shell. Cut fruit into cubes after discarding core.

- While chicken cooks, prepare rice according to package directions. Add 2 cups pineapple cubes, for the last 3 minutes of cooking time.

- Fill the pineapple shells with rice mixture and place half a chicken breast on top of each. Drizzle with sauce.

Honey Glazed Salmon with Black Bean Salsa

Yield: 6 servings

Salmon

½   cup honey
2   tablespoons balsamic vinegar
3   tablespoons vegetable oil, divided

6   salmon fillets (with skin)
Salt and pepper

Black Bean Salsa

1   (15¼-ounce) can black beans, rinsed
    and drained
1   (15¼-ounce) can corn, drained
¼   cup diced celery
¼   cup chopped red onion
1   tablespoon chopped fresh parsley
    or cilantro

⅓   cup thick tomato salsa
2   tablespoons lime juice
2   tablespoons red wine vinegar
1   tablespoon Dijon mustard
1   teaspoon cumin
2   tablespoons vegetable oil

- ■ Stir the honey, vinegar and 1 tablespoon oil in a small saucepan. Bring to a boil and cook, stirring often, until sauce is reduced by half.

- ■ Warm 2 tablespoons of oil in a non-stick frying pan over medium high heat. Season salmon with salt and pepper and place skin side down in the pan. Brush tops with honey mixture and cook for 5 to 8 minutes. Turn salmon and brush the other side with the honey mixture. Cook turning and basting fillets with the honey mixture for approximately 10 minutes.

- ■ For black bean salsa, combine beans, corn, celery, onion and parsley with the tomato salsa.

- ■ Thoroughly mix lime juice, vinegar, mustard and cumin with the oil. Pour over bean mixture.

- ■ Serve salsa over salmon.

Poppy Seed Seared Salmon with Fresh Mango Salsa

Mahi Mah's

Yield: 4 servings

Salmon

4 (6-ounce) salmon steaks
Salt
Black pepper
½ cup poppy seeds
Olive oil
Chopped fresh chives for garnish

Mango Salsa

2 ripe mangoes, peeled and thinly sliced
½ red onion, peeled and thinly sliced
½ red pepper, thinly sliced
4 green onions, white end removed and finely chopped
Salt
Black pepper
1 cup olive oil
1 cup rice wine vinegar

- Season salmon steaks with salt and pepper and coat evenly with poppy seeds.

- Sear fillets in a pan with olive oil over medium-high heat. Cook for 3 minutes per side.

- For salsa, combine mango slices, red onion, red pepper and green onion. Season to taste with salt and pepper.

- Pour olive oil and rice wine vinegar over the mango mixture and toss well. For best flavor allow salsa to sit for 2 hours before serving.

- Top the salmon fillets with salsa and garnish with chives.

Almond Crusted Salmon with Leek and Roasted Garlic Sauce

Steinhilber's Thalia Acres Inn

Yield: 6 servings

4	tablespoons butter, divided	1	cup sliced almonds
3	leeks, halved and thinly sliced	2	tablespoons finely chopped parsley
1	tablespoon fresh lemon juice	1	tablespoon grated lemon peel
1	cup heavy cream	½	cup flour
3	cloves roasted garlic	6	(6-ounce) salmon fillets
Salt		1	egg, beaten
Black pepper		2	tablespoons olive oil

- Melt half the butter in a saucepan over medium-high heat. Sauté leeks for 2 minutes, cover and reduce heat. Cook until leeks are very tender, approximately 20 minutes. Increase heat to medium and mix in lemon juice and cream. Cook for 2 minutes.

- Cool slightly and pour sauce in a blender. Add roasted garlic and purée until smooth. Strain the sauce, extracting as much liquid as possible. Season with salt and pepper and keep warm.

- Chop the sliced almonds and mix them with the parsley, grated lemon peel, salt and pepper.

- Place almond mixture on one plate and flour on another. Season salmon fillets with salt and pepper and dredge the fillets in the flour. Brush the top side of each fillet with the egg wash. Press this brushed side of the fillets into the almond mixture.

- Heat olive oil and remaining butter in a sauté pan over medium heat. Place salmon in the pan, almond-side down and cook until crust is brown, approximately 5 minutes. Turn salmon and finish cooking for 5 to 10 minutes more, until done.

The earth is the Lord's, and everything in it, the world, and all who live in it.

Psalm 24:1

*B*AKED *S*TUFFED *S*EA *B*ASS *A*MANDINE

Yield: 6 servings

Sea Bass

1	sea bass or other whole fish, about 6 pounds, head, tail and backbone removed	⅓	cup butter
2	teaspoons salt, divided	2	tablespoons fresh dill or 2 teaspoons dried
¼	teaspoon pepper, divided	4	cups breadcrumbs
1	chopped onion	2	tablespoons capers
¼	cup chopped celery	6	slices bacon, divided
			Lemon slices for garnish
			Radishes for garnish

Amandine Sauce

¼	cup melted butter	2	tablespoons lemon juice
¼	cup slivered almonds, toasted	¼	cup chopped parsley

▪ Preheat oven to 350 degrees. Wash the prepared fish and pat dry. Sprinkle salt and pepper on the inside using half the salt and a pinch of pepper.

▪ Sauté onion and celery in butter, if using dried dill add it now. Pour this mixture into a bowl with breadcrumbs, capers, fresh dill and remaining salt and pepper. Toss well.

▪ Place stuffing on one side of the fish and fold the other side over; secure with skewers and string. Lay 4 strips of bacon in bottom of a roasting pan. Set fish on the bacon and top with remaining bacon slices.

▪ Bake 18 minutes per pound of fish, basting often with pan drippings. Remove cooked fish to a heated platter and discard bacon.

▪ For the sauce, combine melted butter, toasted almonds and lemon juice.

▪ Pour sauce over the fish and sprinkle with parsley. Garnish with lemon slices and radishes.

CRAB-FILLED ROCKFISH

LUCKY STAR

Yield: 6 servings

1	pound blue crabmeat or lobster meat	3-4	tablespoons flour
6	tablespoons butter, divided	2	tablespoons brandy
1	shallot, finely diced	1	tablespoon Madeira
4	tablespoons washed, thinly sliced leeks		Chicken stock, as needed
1	tablespoon chopped parsley	¼	teaspoon cayenne pepper
2	roasted red peppers, chopped	¼	teaspoon white pepper
		1	teaspoon coarse salt
		1½-2	pounds rockfish fillet

- ■ Pick through crabmeat and refrigerate until needed.

- ■ Heat a large, heavy gauge sauté pan over medium-high heat. Add 3 tablespoons butter. When melted sauté the shallots and leeks, add the parsley and roasted red peppers and sauté another minute. Stir in flour and cook one minute, stirring constantly.

- ■ Remove pan from heat and pour in brandy. Flame the liquor and return the pan to the heat. Stir in Madeira, cayenne pepper and white pepper. If necessary, add just enough chicken stock to moisten. Reduce heat to low and simmer until sauce thickens. Season sauce to taste with salt and let cool. When cool, stir enough sauce into the crabmeat to generously coat.

- ■ Preheat oven to 425 degrees.

- ■ Cut a large pocket in the rockfish fillet. Fill pocket with crab filling. Place stuffed fillet in an ovenproof baking dish. Brush with 3 tablespoons melted butter and season with salt and pepper.

- ■ Bake 20 minutes or until done. Carefully lift fish onto a platter or serve directly from the baking dish.

Taste and see that the Lord is good; blessed is the man who takes refuge in him!

Psalm 34:8

Rockfish à la Willis

Yield: determined by size of fish

Rockfish
Mayonnaise to cover the fish
½ lemon
Salt and pepper to taste
Old Bay seasoning to taste

½ onion, sliced
1-2 red, yellow or green bell peppers, sliced
½ mango or pineapple, sliced

- Cover the fish with mayonnaise (the more mayonnaise, the moister the fish).

- Squeeze the juice of the lemon over the fish. Add salt and pepper and Old Bay seasoning to taste.

- Layer onion, bell pepper and mango or pineapple slices on the fish.

- Wrap the fish in foil tightly enclosed.

- Place on a covered grill for 1 to 1½ hours on low heat.

Fillet of Sole with Tarragon and Garlic

Yield: 4 servings

6 tablespoons butter or margarine, divided
1 cup sliced, blanched garlic
1½ pounds sole fillets
All-purpose flour to coat fillets
2 tablespoons vegetable oil

¼ cup white wine vinegar
1½ teaspoons dry or 1½ tablespoons fresh tarragon
Tarragon or parsley for garnish
Lemon wedges

- In a 12 to 14-inch skillet melt 4 tablespoons butter over medium heat. Add the sliced, blanched garlic and sauté until pale gold, not brown, for approximately 5 minutes. Remove garlic from the pan and keep warm.

- Coat the sole fillets with flour and shake off excess. Add the remaining butter and the oil to the pan on medium-high heat. When bubbling add fillets to the pan. Be careful not to crowd them.

- Cook fillets for 3 to 5 minutes, turning once. Fish should be golden brown and flaky. Remove fillets to a platter and keep warm.

- Add the vinegar and tarragon to the pan drippings. Boil the liquid on high heat until it is reduced to 3 tablespoons, about 1 minute. Drizzle this sauce over the fillets and top with the sautéed garlic. Garnish with tarragon or parsley and lemon wedges.

BAKED RED SNAPPER

Yield: 3 to 4 servings

Red Snapper

1	(3 to 4-pound) red snapper (not fillets)	2	cups coarsely chopped parsley
Melted butter		2	dozen baby carrots or 5 to 6 carrots, cut in strips
Salt			
Pepper		8	scallions
4	stalks celery, cut in long pieces		

Stuffing

2	onions, diced	2	cups breadcrumbs
⅓	cup butter, melted	¼	teaspoon sage
½	cup finely chopped mushrooms	¼	teaspoon oregano
		½	teaspoon salt
2	tablespoons minced parsley	¼	teaspoon black pepper
		½	cup pale dry sherry

- Preheat oven to 375 degrees.

- Wash fish and pat dry with paper towels. Brush fish inside and out with melted butter. Season to taste with salt and pepper.

- Prepare stuffing by sautéing the onion in butter until just tender. Stir in the mushrooms, minced parsley, breadcrumbs, sage, oregano, salt, pepper and sherry. Blend thoroughly.

- Stuff fish with mixture and cover the opening with foil.

- Place celery, parsley, carrots and scallions into a 9 x 13 x 2-inch baking dish and sprinkle with salt and pepper. Set stuffed snapper on top of vegetables and bake until flaky, about 25 to 30 minutes.

Come Lord Jesus,
Be our Guest,
And let this food,
To us be blessed.
Amen.

One of the four prayers said by Barbara Principe's daughters.

Signature Fried Oysters

Princess Anne Country Club

Yield: 4 servings

Vegetable or canola oil for deep fat frying
1 quart freshly shucked raw oysters
3 cups flour
Salt and pepper to taste
8 eggs, beaten

1 cup light cream
1 cup grated Parmesan cheese
3 cups unseasoned breadcrumbs
1½ tablespoons roasted garlic powder
1 tablespoon seafood seasoning

- Fill deep fat fryer and heat to 375 degrees.
- Drain oysters and dredge through flour that has been seasoned with salt and pepper.
- Combine beaten eggs with cream for egg wash. In a shallow pan, stir together Parmesan cheese, breadcrumbs, roasted garlic powder, seasoning, salt and pepper.
- Dip oysters in egg wash one at a time, then coat with the bread crumb mixture.
- Deep fry until golden brown, 2 to 3 minutes. Drain and serve with cocktail and/or tartare sauce.

Scalloped Oysters

Travis House

Yield: 8 to 10 servings

1 quart oysters
½ cup butter
½ cup flour
1½ teaspoons paprika
1 teaspoon salt
¼ teaspoon black pepper
Dash red pepper

Dash sugar
1 green pepper, finely chopped
1 onion, finely chopped
½ teaspoon minced garlic
1 teaspoon lemon juice
1 tablespoon Worcestershire sauce

- Preheat oven to 400 degrees.
- Melt butter in large skillet. Add flour and cook until light brown, stirring constantly. Stir in paprika, salt, black pepper, red pepper and sugar. Mix in green pepper, onion and garlic and sauté for 5 minutes.
- Remove pan from heat and pour in lemon juice, Worcestershire and oysters that have been heated (not cooked) in their own liquor. Mix well and place in a 2 to 3-quart baking dish. Sprinkle breadcrumbs over the top.
- Bake for 30 minutes.

Cioppino

Yield: Depends on amount of seafood

1 large onion, minced	1 teaspoon dried oregano
½ cup chopped celery	1 teaspoon dried thyme
½ cup chopped green pepper	1 teaspoon dried parsley
2 cloves garlic, minced	6 peppercorns
½ cup vegetable oil	1 bay leaf
1 (16-ounce) can whole tomatoes	Raw clams
1 (8-ounce) can tomato sauce	Raw shrimp
1 cup white wine (never red)	Scallops
1 teaspoon dried basil	Sea bass, etc.

■ Sauté the onion, celery, green pepper and garlic in the oil until translucent. Add the tomatoes, tomato sauce, wine, basil, oregano, thyme, parsley, peppercorns and bay leaf. Simmer the sauce for 1 to 2 hours.

■ Preheat oven to 300 degrees. In a large roasting pan layer several different kinds of your favorite seafood. Pour the hot tomato sauce over the layered seafood and cover tightly. Bake for 1 to 1½ hours, stirring after 45 minutes. Turn off oven and leave in the oven until serving.

10 pounds clams, 6 pounds sea bass, 4 pounds shrimp and 4 crabs will serve 20.

Mussels Diablo

Coyote Café

Yield: 2 servings

3 tablespoons olive oil	1 tablespoon salt
1 jalapeño pepper, sliced	1 tablespoon black pepper
1 tablespoon fresh minced garlic	3 dozen fresh mussels
4 leaves fresh sage, chopped	¾ cup white wine
1 cup canned or fresh tomatoes	

■ Heat a large pan on high heat and add olive oil, jalapeño pepper and garlic. Sauté until the garlic is golden brown.

■ Quickly add the sage, tomatoes, salt, pepper and mussels (about 30 seconds). Add the white wine and cover. Turn heat down to medium-low and continue heating for approximately 2 minutes, or until all mussels have opened.

Chef Mark McConnell suggests serving this with French bread.

Pasta with Scallops

Yield: 2 servings

1 teaspoon black peppercorns, coarsely ground
¾ pound sea scallops
Olive oil for sautéing
2 green onions, chopped with tops
1 clove garlic, minced
2 tablespoons capers
¼ cup sliced ripe olives
2 Roma tomatoes, coarsely chopped
¼ cup white wine
¼ teaspoon crushed red pepper
Salt
Pepper
Lemon wedges
8 ounces cooked fettuccini
Chopped parsley for garnish

- Press peppercorns into scallops.

- Heat 1 to 2 tablespoons olive oil in a skillet. Sauté scallops over medium heat for 2 to 3 minutes until barely done. Remove scallops and keep warm.

- Sauté green onions and garlic for 1 minute, adding olive oil to the skillet if needed. Stir in capers, olives, tomatoes and wine. Season with red pepper and salt and pepper to taste.

- Turn heat to high; cook tomato mixture until slightly thickened, about 2 minutes.

- Reduce heat and return scallops to skillet, stirring into tomato mixture. Serve over linguine with lemon wedges. Garnish with parsley.

Shrimp, Shallots and Chardonnay

Yield: 4 to 6 servings

2 cups Chardonnay
2 shallots, minced
4 tablespoons butter
¼ teaspoon cayenne pepper
2 pounds shrimp, shelled and deveined
Chopped parsley for garnish

- Cook Chardonnay, shallots, butter and cayenne pepper in a large skillet until liquid is reduced to a small amount.

- Gently stir in shrimp and cook over low heat until shrimp are just cooked through, for 3 to 5 minutes. Sprinkle with parsley.

Baked Shrimp in Shell

Yield: 2 servings

1	pound shrimp	1	teaspoon salt
3	tablespoons olive oil	1	lemon, squeezed
1	clove garlic, minced		Freshly ground pepper
1	tablespoon Worcestershire sauce	2	tablespoons butter or margarine

- Preheat oven to 350 degrees.

- Wash shrimp, drain. Place in single layer in a large baking dish.

- Combine olive oil, garlic, Worcestershire sauce, salt, lemon and pepper. Pour over shrimp. Dot with butter.

- Bake for 20 minutes, stirring occasionally.

- Serve sauce in individual bowls for dipping with French bread.

Drunken Butterfly Shrimp

Yield: 4 servings

⅓	cup dry vermouth	1	pound large shrimp, peeled
1	teaspoon instant chicken-flavored bouillon	1	egg
¼	teaspoon salt	½	cup flour
⅛	teaspoon pepper	3	tablespoons olive oil
½	cup water	2	teaspoons minced parsley
			Lemon slices for garnish

- Mix vermouth, bouillon, salt and pepper with water in a measuring cup. Set aside.

- Butterfly peeled shrimp by cutting each shrimp ¾ of way through along center back; spread shrimp open. Rinse under cold water to remove vein. Pat dry with paper towels.

- In an 8 or 9-inch pie plate, beat the egg with a fork. Measure flour onto waxed paper. Dip shrimp in egg then in flour to coat.

- Heat oil in skillet over medium heat until hot and bubbly. Cook shrimp until lightly browned on both sides. Remove shrimp to a plate as they brown.

- Return shrimp to skillet and stir in vermouth mixture. Heat to boiling over medium-high heat for 1 minute to blend flavors, stirring occasionally. Spoon shrimp and sauce onto platter. Sprinkle with chopped parsley and garnish with lemon slices.

Wonderful Shrimp

Yield: 4 servings

1	stick butter	1	tablespoon sugar
¼	cup cooking sherry or red cooking wine	1	pound raw shrimp, peeled and deveined
2	teaspoons Worcestershire sauce	¼	cup minced fresh parsley
1	clove garlic, minced	1	tablespoon grated Parmesan cheese
2	tablespoons fresh lemon juice		

- Preheat broiler. Melt butter in a 12 x 9-inch baking dish. Add sherry or wine, Worcestershire sauce, garlic, lemon juice and sugar to dish. Mix well.

- Lay raw shrimp in baking dish in a single layer. Broil for 8 minutes. Remove from oven and allow to stand for 15 minutes. Sprinkle parsley over the shrimp and return to broiler for 3 minutes. Remove and sprinkle Parmesan over the top.

This dish is a delicious appetizer as well as an entrée.

Sesame Shrimp and Asparagus

Yield: 6 servings

1½	pounds large shrimp	2	small onions, sliced
1½	pounds asparagus	4	teaspoons soy sauce
1	tablespoon sesame seeds	1	teaspoon salt (optional)
Olive oil to cover pan			

- Shell and devein shrimp. Discard tough ends and trim scales from asparagus. Cut asparagus into 2-inch pieces. Set shrimp and asparagus aside.

- In large skillet over medium heat, toast sesame seeds until golden, stirring and shaking skillet occasionally. Remove seeds to small bowl and set aside.

- Pour enough olive oil to cover bottom of same skillet. Over medium-high heat cook asparagus, onions and shrimp until shrimp are pink and vegetables are tender-crisp. Stir frequently for about 5 minutes. Add sesame seeds, soy sauce and salt and stir until just mixed.

SHRIMP CREOLE

Yield: 8 servings

2	pieces bacon, cooked and crumbled	1	teaspoon sugar
1	small onion, chopped	2	tablespoons chopped parsley
1	cup chopped celery		Salt
½	cup chopped green pepper		Pepper
1	(16-ounce) can tomatoes	2	tablespoons cornstarch, optional
1	(16-ounce) can tomato sauce	1	pound cooked shrimp

- Cook bacon and reserve grease. Sauté onion and celery in bacon grease until tender.

- Add bacon, green pepper, tomatoes, tomato sauce, sugar and parsley. Season to taste with salt and pepper. Simmer uncovered for 45 minutes. If mixture is not thick enough mix 2 tablespoons cornstarch in 1 tablespoon water and add to sauce.

- Stir in cooked shrimp and serve hot over rice.

SHRIMP SCAMPI

Yield: 4 servings

1½	sticks butter	1	pound shrimp, shelled
¼	cup finely chopped onion	¼	cup white wine
3	cloves garlic, crushed or 1 tablespoon minced garlic	2	tablespoons lemon juice
4	parsley sprigs, chopped		

- Melt the butter and sauté the onions, garlic and parsley for 10 minutes. Stir in uncooked shrimp and add wine and lemon juice.

- Simmer until shrimp turn pink.

SHRIMP ATLANTICA

Yield: 4 servings

½	cup finely chopped onion	1	teaspoon white pepper
½	cup olive oil, divided	1	teaspoon black pepper
3	cups diced fresh tomatoes, skinned and seeded		Pinch of cayenne pepper
		1	pound linguini
2	teaspoons sugar	20	large shrimp, peeled and deveined
2	tablespoons minced garlic	2	tablespoons chopped fresh parsley
1	teaspoon chopped fresh basil	8	large pitted black olives, sliced
1	teaspoon chopped fresh oregano	2	tablespoons capers
1	teaspoon chopped fresh marjoram	¼	cup grated Romano cheese
1	teaspoon coarse salt		

- Lightly brown the onion in ¼ cup olive oil. Add tomatoes, sugar, garlic, basil, oregano, marjoram, salt, white pepper, black pepper and cayenne pepper. Simmer over low heat for 1½ hours, stirring occasionally.

- Bring one gallon of salted water to a boil and cook linguini until al dente, about 8 to 10 minutes. Just before pasta is done, add shrimp to the red sauce and cook for 4 minutes.

- Drain pasta and toss with ¼ cup olive oil and parsley in a large bowl.

- Divide onto plates and top pasta with shrimp sauce. Garnish with olives, capers and cheese.

SHRIMP AND CRABMEAT GUMBO

Yield: 16 servings

¾ cup vegetable oil
¾ cup flour
2 cups chopped onion
½ cup chopped green pepper
½ cup finely chopped green onion tops
2 tablespoons minced parsley
1 tablespoon minced garlic
2 large tomatoes, chopped
1¼ pounds smoked sausage, cut into ½-inch slices
2½ quarts water, divided

2 pounds whole shrimp, peeled and deveined, divided
1 pound crabmeat
5 teaspoons salt
3 whole bay leaves, crushed
½ teaspoon dried thyme
1¼ teaspoons freshly ground black pepper
¼ teaspoon cayenne pepper
4 teaspoons lemon juice
10 whole allspice
½ teaspoon mace
8 whole cloves

- Heat oil in a 7 to 8-quart stockpot. Add flour and make a roux, cook 20 to 30 minutes until browned.

- Immediately add the onion, green pepper, green onion tops, parsley and garlic. Continue cooking for 10 minutes.

- Add tomatoes and sausage; mix thoroughly. Add 2 quarts water, 1 pound raw shrimp, crabmeat, salt, bay leaves, thyme, black pepper, cayenne pepper, lemon juice, allspice, mace and cloves. Bring to a boil, then lower heat and simmer for 1 hour, occasionally stirring and scraping sides and bottom to avoid scorching.

- Add remaining ½-quart water and pound of shrimp. Simmer 10 to 12 minutes until shrimp turn pink. Stir thoroughly; turn off heat and cover.

- Let rest, covered, for 15 minutes before serving over rice.

Fear the Lord, you his saints, for those who fear Him lack nothing.

Psalm 34:9

DEVILED CRABS

Yield: 8 servings

1	pound crabmeat	½	teaspoon dry mustard
1	cup coarse breadcrumbs	½	teaspoon salt
½	cup minced celery	¼	teaspoon pepper
¼	cup minced green pepper	¼	teaspoon hot pepper sauce
2	eggs, beaten	½	cup mayonnaise
2	tablespoons lemon juice	½	cup melted butter
1	teaspoon vinegar	1	tablespoon Worcestershire sauce

- Preheat oven to 375 degrees. Butter 8 crab shells or ramekins.

- Mix crabmeat, breadcrumbs, celery, green pepper and eggs.

- Combine lemon juice, vinegar, mustard, salt, pepper and hot pepper sauce with the mayonnaise and blend well. Stir in butter, a little at a time. Pour over the crabmeat mixture and mix thoroughly.

- Bake for about 8 minutes until lightly browned.

CRAB AU GRATIN

Yield: 6 servings

6	tablespoons butter, divided	1	teaspoon Worcestershire sauce
4	tablespoons flour	1	tablespoon lemon juice
1	teaspoon salt	1	pound crabmeat
½	teaspoon white pepper	2	tablespoons sherry
1¾	cups milk		Dash red pepper
½	cup light cream	1	cup soft breadcrumbs
1½	cups shredded sharp cheese		

- Preheat oven to 425 degrees. Butter a 1½-quart casserole dish.

- Melt 4 tablespoons butter and stir in flour to make a roux. Add salt and pepper. Stir in milk and cream slowly, whisking until sauce thickens. Mix in cheese, Worcestershire sauce, lemon juice and crabmeat. Add sherry and red pepper to taste.

- Pour into prepared dish and bake for 15 minutes. Add remaining 2 tablespoons of melted butter to breadcrumbs and sprinkle over the top. Bake another 10 minutes.

Entrées—Seafood

CRABMEAT BUNGALOW

Yield: 5 to 6 servings

3	slices white bread	2	tablespoons dry sherry
2	eggs	1	pound lump crabmeat
1	teaspoon Worcestershire sauce	2	sticks butter, melted
1/3	teaspoon ground red pepper	2	tablespoons fresh chopped parsley
1/3	teaspoon baking powder		Salt to taste
1	(12-ounce) can evaporated milk		

- Preheat oven to 350 degrees. Butter a 2½-quart covered casserole dish.

- Soak bread slices in water; press dry and tear into pieces.

- Beat eggs and add Worcestershire sauce, red pepper, baking powder, milk and sherry. Mix well. Pour liquid mixture into prepared casserole dish.

- Add crabmeat, bread, butter, parsley, and salt. Stir gently.

- Bake for 1 hour until firm. Cover for the last 10 to 15 minutes if it browns too quickly.

HAWAIIAN BAKED AVOCADO AND CRABMEAT

Yield: 2 servings

6	ounces crabmeat	2	tablespoons breadcrumbs
2	tablespoons grated Romano cheese	1	large avocado, ripe but not soft
2	teaspoons chopped parsley	2	pats butter

- Preheat oven to 325 degrees.

- Mix crabmeat, Romano cheese, parsley and breadcrumbs.

- Cut avocado in half and remove seed. Slice a small amount off the bottom of each half so avocado sits level.

- Spoon crabmeat mixture into the avocado halves, leaving rounded peaks. Sprinkle a few extra breadcrumbs on each half with a pat of butter.

- Place on cookie sheet and bake for 10 to 15 minutes.

CRAB IMPERIAL

Yield: 8 servings

3	tablespoons butter		Dash of pepper
2	tablespoons chopped onion	1	cup milk
3	tablespoons flour	½	cup heavy cream
1	teaspoon dry mustard	½	cup shredded Cheddar cheese
½	teaspoon paprika	3	cups crabmeat
¾	teaspoon salt	½	cup buttered breadcrumbs

- Preheat oven to 350 degrees.

- Melt butter in a saucepan; add onions and sauté until translucent. Add flour, mustard, paprika, salt and pepper to the onions and mix. Stir constantly and slowly pour in milk. Add cream, cheese and crabmeat to the sauce and blend.

- Fill buttered crab shells or casserole dish and top with buttered breadcrumbs. Bake for 20 to 30 minutes until browned.

CHESAPEAKE STYLE CRABCAKES

Yield: 8 servings

1	pound crabmeat	1	teaspoon mayonnaise
8	saltine crackers, crushed	1	teaspoon seafood seasoning
1	egg		Olive oil for frying
1	teaspoon mustard		

- Combine crabmeat, cracker crumbs, egg, mustard, mayonnaise and seafood seasoning. Shape into cakes.

- Refrigerate or freeze crabcakes for 20 to 30 minutes.

- Fry in hot olive oil until golden brown.

STUFFED EGGPLANT WITH CRABMEAT

Yield: 2 servings

1 large eggplant	Salt and pepper
2 tablespoons chopped shallots or green onions	½ cup lump crabmeat
	½ cup chopped, cooked shrimp
1 teaspoon parsley	Grated Parmesan cheese
4 tablespoons butter	French breadcrumbs

■ Preheat oven to 375 degrees.

■ Cut eggplant in half lengthwise and bake until tender. Scoop out pulp.

■ Decrease oven temperature to 350 degrees.

■ Sauté shallots and parsley in butter. Season to taste with salt and pepper and add eggplant pulp, crabmeat and shrimp. Stir and cook 3 to 4 minutes. Spoon mixture into eggplant shells. Top with Parmesan cheese and breadcrumbs.

■ Brown in oven.

CRAB CASSEROLE I

Yield: 8 servings

½ pound fresh mushrooms, sliced	½ cup light cream
2 teaspoons butter	¼ teaspoon pepper
½ pound wild rice, not instant	½ teaspoon Worcestershire sauce
1 (10¾-ounce) can cream of mushroom soup	1½ pounds crabmeat
	1 cup shredded Cheddar cheese

■ Preheat oven to 350 degrees.

■ Sauté mushrooms in butter. Cook rice according to package directions.

■ Dilute the mushroom soup with the light cream and add pepper and Worcestershire sauce.

■ In a 2½-quart covered casserole dish, layer the rice, mushrooms, crabmeat and soup mixture. Cover the top with shredded cheese.

■ Bake covered for 30 minutes. Uncover and return to oven until cheese is melted and lightly browned.

CRAB CASSEROLE *II*

Yield: 4 to 6 servings

1 pound crabmeat	Salt and pepper
1 stalk celery, finely chopped	Worcestershire sauce
1 teaspoon dried parsley	3 slices toast
2 hard-cooked eggs, chopped	Butter
1 (10¾-ounce) can cream of mushroom soup	Breadcrumbs

- Combine crabmeat, celery, parsley, eggs and mushroom soup. Season to taste with salt, pepper and Worcestershire sauce.

- Lay toast slices in the bottom of a 9 x 13 x 3-inch baking dish. Spoon crabmeat mixture over toast. Top with butter and breadcrumbs and bake for 1 hour.

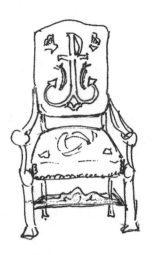

Spinach Pie

Yield: 6 to 8 servings

1	cup shredded sharp Cheddar cheese, packed gently	2	(10-ounce) packages frozen chopped spinach
½	teaspoon salt	1	(8-ounce) package cream cheese
¼	teaspoon dry mustard	½	cup fine breadcrumbs
½	cup softened butter, divided	¼	cup melted butter
¾	cup flour	½	teaspoon ground sage

- Preheat oven to 350 degrees.

- For crust, combine the shredded cheese, salt, mustard, half the softened butter and flour. Mix with a fork until mixture is crumbly. Press into a 9-inch pie pan. Bake for 10 minutes.

- Cook spinach according to package directions. Drain well and squeeze out liquid. Mix the spinach with cream cheese and remaining softened butter. Pour mixture into the crust.

- Combine breadcrumbs, melted butter and sage. Sprinkle over top of the pie.

- Bake for 20 to 30 minutes.

Pat Mann's daughter, Mary Ernst, won first place with this recipe in a newspaper contest in Sun Prairie, Wisconsin.

Broccoli and Ziti

Aldo's

Yield: 6 to 8 servings

1	pound uncooked ziti pasta	1	cup chicken broth
6-8	cloves garlic, chopped		Crushed red pepper (optional)
¾	cup olive oil		Salt
¼	cup sliced cherry peppers, hot or mild		Pepper
2	heads broccoli, cut into florets and lightly blanched		Parmesan cheese

- Cook ziti pasta al dente.

- Pour olive oil in a large skillet. Sauté garlic and cherry peppers and broccoli for several minutes. Add chicken broth and bring to a simmer, seasoning with crushed red pepper, salt and pepper.

- Drain cooked pasta and return it to the pot. Combine broccoli mixture with ziti and toss. Pour into serving bowl and sprinkle with Parmesan cheese.

PORTOBELLO PENNE

Yield: 4 servings

12 ounces penne pasta	1 pound portobello mushrooms, sliced
3 large Vidalia onions, chopped	Freshly ground black pepper
1 tablespoon unsalted butter, divided	4 ounces goat cheese, crumbled
2½ tablespoons olive oil, divided	2 tablespoons freshly grated
½ teaspoon sugar	Parmesan cheese
¾ teaspoon salt, divided	

- Boil penne about 10 minutes or until al dente. Reserve 1 cup of the pasta water; drain the pasta.

- While pasta cooks, sauté onions in ½ the butter and 1 tablespoon of olive oil. Stir in sugar and ½ teaspoon salt. Cook over medium heat until onions are tender and browned, about 15 to 20 minutes, stirring frequently. Remove to bowl.

- While onions are cooking, clean mushrooms and remove stems. Cut caps in half and slice ¼-inch thick. Melt remaining butter and 1 tablespoon of olive oil in same skillet. Sauté mushrooms with ¼ teaspoon salt for 5 minutes or until tender and browned, stirring frequently. Add the reserved onions and season to taste with pepper.

- Toss penne with ¾ cup reserved pasta water, mushroom-onion mixture, crumbled goat cheese, Parmesan cheese and ½ tablespoon olive oil. Add more pasta water and/or olive oil if pasta seems dry. Serve immediately with more Parmesan cheese and pepper.

ASPARAGUS FETTUCCINI

Yield: 4 servings

6 tablespoons butter	Salt
1½ pounds asparagus	Pepper
1 pound fettuccini, cooked and drained	Freshly grated Parmesan cheese

- Slowly brown the butter in a pan.

- Steam asparagus until tender, not limp.

- Place asparagus in the pan with butter, then add to freshly cooked fettuccini. Season with salt and pepper. Sprinkle Parmesan on top.

VEGETABLE LASAGNA

Yield: 8 to 9 servings

2	cups grated zucchini	2½	cups spaghetti sauce, divided
2	cups grated carrots		
1	tablespoon olive oil, divided	½	pound lasagna noodles, cooked
3	eggs	8	ounces shredded mozzarella or provolone cheese, divided
1	cup Parmesan cheese, divided		
2	(10-ounce) packages chopped spinach, thawed and squeezed to drain		

■ Preheat oven to 350 degrees.

■ Sauté zucchini and carrots separately, each in ½ tablespoon of olive oil until tender, but crisp.

■ Combine the eggs and Parmesan cheese, dividing the egg mixture into 3 bowls. Stir the carrots, zucchini and spinach into the egg mixture, each vegetable in a separate bowl.

■ Spoon ⅔ cup of spaghetti sauce into lasagna baking dish. Place ½ the noodles over the sauce. Spread spinach mixture over the noodles and top with ⅓ of the shredded cheese. Follow this with the carrot mixture, ⅔ cup of sauce and ⅓ of the shredded cheese, then the zucchini mixture.

■ Top with remaining noodles and sauce.

■ Cover with foil and bake for 30 minutes.

■ Remove the foil and top with the remaining cheese. Cook an additional 10 minutes uncovered. Cool at least 15 minutes before cutting.

Trust in the Lord, and do good; dwell in the land, and enjoy safe pasture. Delight yourself in the Lord, and he will give you the desires of your heart.

Psalm 37:3-4

*T*EMPEH *T*ACOS

Yield: 4 servings

8-12 taco shells
1 (8-ounce) package tempeh
¼ cup olive oil
1 clove garlic, crushed
½ onion, chopped
½ (1-ounce) package taco seasoning

1 cup water
Lettuce, shredded
Tomato, chopped
1 cup shredded Cheddar cheese
Sour cream
Salsa

- Preheat oven to 350 degrees. Heat taco shells for 5 minutes.
- In a skillet, crumble tempeh into olive oil. Stir in crushed garlic and onions and brown.
- Add taco seasoning to skillet. Add water as needed.
- Spoon into taco shells with lettuce, tomatoes, shredded cheese and sour cream and/or salsa.

*L*AYERED *V*EGETABLE *C*HEESE *B*AKE

Yield: 6 side servings or 4 main servings

1 tablespoon vegetable oil
1 large onion, coarsely chopped
1 large green pepper, seeded and chopped
1 eggplant, peeled and cut into 1-inch cubes
½ pound mushrooms, sliced

1 large tomato, chopped
¾ teaspoon dried thyme
⅛ teaspoon pepper
1 cup packaged herb-seasoned stuffing mix
1 (8-ounce) brick Swiss cheese, coarsely shredded and divided

- Preheat oven to 350 degrees. Grease a 2½ to 3-quart baking dish.
- In a large skillet, heat oil over medium heat. Stir in onion and green pepper and sauté for 3 minutes. Add eggplant and mushrooms stirring constantly. Stir in tomato, thyme and pepper and cook 1 minute.
- Spread dry stuffing mix over the bottom of prepared baking dish. Layer half the vegetable mixture and half the cheese over the stuffing. Top with remaining vegetable mixture.
- Cover and bake for 30 minutes.
- Sprinkle with remaining half of the cheese and bake uncovered for 10 minutes more or until cheese melts.

Tomato Basil Pasta

Yield: 6 servings

4   large tomatoes, chopped
1   cup fresh basil, cut
¾   cup olive oil
3   cloves garlic, minced
1   pound feta cheese or fresh mozzarella

1   teaspoon salt
Dash pepper
1½   pounds linguine noodles, cooked and drained

- Mix tomatoes, basil, olive oil, garlic, cheese, salt and pepper in a large bowl.
- Let mixture set at room temperature for 2½ hours.
- Toss with freshly cooked noodles.

This makes a good summer meal when served with salad and focaccia.

Zucchini in Alfredo Sauce

Yield: 8 servings

5   large zucchini (about 2½ pounds)
1   teaspoon salt
2-3 cloves garlic, minced
2   tablespoons olive oil
1   (8-ounce) package cream cheese, cubed and softened

⅔   cup light cream
½   cup finely shredded Parmesan cheese, divided
Coarsely ground black pepper
Ground nutmeg

- Cut zucchini into ¼-inch wide and ¼-inch thick strips. Place the zucchini in a colander and toss with the salt. Rinse, drain for 1 hour and pat dry.
- Cook the zucchini and garlic in hot oil in a 12-inch skillet over medium-high heat for 2 to 4 minutes or until crisp and tender. Transfer to a large bowl.
- Heat the cream cheese and cream in the same skillet over medium-low heat until mixture is smooth. Blend in ½ cup Parmesan cheese. Mix in the zucchini and heat thoroughly.
- Transfer to a serving dish. Sprinkle with pepper, nutmeg and additional cheese.

Broccoli Impossible Pie

Yield: 6 servings

2	cups chopped fresh broccoli	¾	cup biscuit baking mix
½	cup chopped onion	3	eggs, beaten
½	cup chopped green onion	1	teaspoon salt
1	cup shredded cheese	¼	teaspoon pepper
1½	cups milk		

- Preheat oven to 400 degrees. Grease a 9-inch pie plate.
- Cook and drain broccoli. Combine broccoli, onions, cheese, milk, biscuit baking mix, eggs, salt and pepper.
- Pour mixture into prepared pie plate and bake for 35 to 40 minutes.

Cauliflower may be substituted for broccoli.

Vegetable Tofu Stir-Fry

Yield: 6 to 8 servings

12-16	ounces tofu	1	cup snow peas
	Soy sauce		Olive oil
1	head broccoli	1	large onion
2	zucchini	½	cup slivered almonds
2	carrots	½	cup bean sprouts
1	stalk celery		

- Drain tofu. Place it in enough soy sauce to cover.
- Cut broccoli, zucchini, carrots and celery into bite-sized pieces. Rinse snow peas and cut them in half.
- Heat 1 tablespoon olive oil in a wok. Add the onion and broccoli pieces to the oil and sauté until the onion is soft. Set aside.
- Add more olive oil to the hot wok. Place the carrots, celery, zucchini, almonds, and bean sprouts in the wok. Stir-fry for 2 minutes.
- Add snow peas and stir for about 30 seconds.
- Drain soy sauce from the tofu and reserve the soy sauce. Cube the tofu.
- Return the broccoli, zucchini, carrots, celery, almonds, bean sprouts and snow peas to the wok with the tofu. Stir-fry for 1 minute. Stir in reserved soy sauce. Cover and cook for 1 to 2 minutes more.
- Serve over rice.

"Beets"
by Hazel Z. Chilton

Vegetables
&
Accompaniments

Vegetables & Accompaniments

Corn Fritters

Yield: 12 fritters

1	cup fresh or drained canned corn	½	teaspoon baking powder
2	eggs, beaten	½	teaspoon nutmeg
6	tablespoons flour		Oil for frying

- Combine corn, eggs, flour, baking powder and nutmeg.
- Drop by tablespoons into very hot oil. Cook until golden and drain on paper towels.

Corn Pudding

Yield: 4 to 6 servings

2	cups fresh corn	2	cups milk or 1 cup milk and 1 cup heavy cream
2	teaspoons flour		Pinch of salt
1	cup sugar		Butter
2	eggs		

- Preheat oven to 350 degrees. Grease a 1½-quart casserole dish.
- Cut or grate corn from cobs. Scrape cobs for additional thickening.
- Mix flour with sugar and add to corn. Add eggs, milk and salt and mix well.
- Pour pudding into prepared casserole dish and dot with butter. Bake for 30 to 45 minutes, stirring 3 to 4 times while baking.

Easy Corn Pudding

Yield: 4 to 5 servings

1	pint cream-style corn	2	tablespoons sugar
3	eggs	1	teaspoon salt
1	cup milk		Butter
3	tablespoons flour		

- Preheat oven to 350 degrees. Grease a 1-quart baking dish.
- Combine corn, eggs, milk, flour, sugar and salt. Mix with electric mixer. Pour into prepared baking dish. Dot with butter.
- Bake for 30 minutes.

This recipe may be baked for 15 to 20 minutes at 425 degrees, until pudding is set and browned.

SWEET POTATOES WITH RUM AND WALNUTS

Yield: 4 to 6 servings

4-6 sweet potatoes or yams	¼ cup walnuts, chopped
⅓ cup brown sugar	3 ounces amber or dark rum
½ teaspoon salt	3 tablespoons butter
¼ teaspoon pepper	

- Preheat oven to 350 degrees. Grease a 2-quart baking dish.

- Boil whole sweet potatoes until just tender. Drain and cool. Remove potato skins and slice potatoes into ½-inch thick slices. Arrange in 2 layers in prepared baking dish, sprinkling each layer with salt, pepper and brown sugar. Sprinkle the top layer with walnuts and rum. Dot generously with butter.

- Bake for 20 minutes until heated through. If desired, more rum can be poured over and flamed.

Cheryl Jordan recommends that this recipe be served with turkey or pork.

SWEET POTATOES IN ORANGE HALVES

Yield: 6 servings

2-3 sweet potatoes, depending on size	½ teaspoon cinnamon
3 oranges, halved	½ teaspoon nutmeg
2 tablespoons butter, softened	½ cup brown sugar

- Preheat oven to 350 degrees. Grease a shallow baking dish.

- Boil sweet potatoes in their skins until tender. Skin while hot. Beat potatoes until mashed.

- Juice the orange halves, straining and reserving juice. Scoop pulp out of halves and set cups aside.

- Stir butter, cinnamon, nutmeg, ¼ cup reserved orange juice and brown sugar into mashed potatoes. Mix well. Spoon mixture into orange cups. Place in prepared baking dish.

- Bake for 20 minutes.

The top of the filled orange halves may be sprinkled with pecans.

Sweet Potato Pudding

Yield: 8 servings

Sweet Potatoes

3	large sweet potatoes, boiled until tender	1	tablespoon vanilla extract
¼	cup sugar	½	cup butter
2	eggs, slightly beaten	½	teaspoon nutmeg

Topping

1	cup brown sugar	1	cup chopped pecans
⅓	cup all-purpose flour	⅓	cup butter, melted

■ Preheat oven to 350 degrees. Grease a 1½-quart baking dish.

■ Combine sweet potatoes, sugar, eggs, vanilla, butter and nutmeg. Mix with electric mixer or blender. Transfer to prepared baking dish.

■ For topping, combine brown sugar, flour and pecans in a pan with the melted butter. Crumble the mixture over sweet potatoes.

■ Bake for 30 minutes.

Grated Sweet Potato Pudding

Yield: 6 servings

2	cups grated uncooked sweet potatoes	1	teaspoon cinnamon
		1	teaspoon nutmeg
1	cup sugar	½	teaspoon ground cloves
½	cup flour	2	cups milk
⅔	cup butter	2	eggs

■ Preheat oven to 350 degrees. Grease a 1½-quart baking dish.

■ Blend sweet potatoes, sugar, flour, butter, cinnamon, nutmeg, cloves, milk and eggs. Place mixture in prepared baking dish.

■ Bake for 1 hour, stirring occasionally.

POTATO AND CARROT CASSEROLE

Yield: 4 servings

8	ounces carrots	1	clove garlic, minced
8	ounces potatoes		Salt
8	ounces onions		Freshly ground black pepper
1-2	ounces butter		

- Preheat oven to 325 degrees. Grease an 8 x 8 x 2-inch baking dish.
- Cut the carrots, potatoes and onions into thin matchstick slivers. Use a mandoline, if available.
- Melt butter in a saucepan and sauté the garlic; do not brown. Stir in carrots, potatoes and onion. Sauté for 5 minutes, stirring constantly. Season to taste with salt and pepper.
- Transfer vegetables to the prepared baking dish. Bake 1 hour and 15 minutes.

GOURMET CREAMED POTATOES

Yield: 8 servings

8-10	medium potatoes, halved		Salt
1	(8-ounce) package cream cheese, softened		Pepper
		2	tablespoons butter
8	ounces sour cream		Paprika

- Preheat oven to 325 degrees. Grease a 1½-quart baking dish.
- Peel and boil potatoes until done when stuck with a fork. Drain potatoes and reserve potato water. Place potatoes in a mixing bowl.
- Add the cream cheese and sour cream and beat with an electric mixer until smooth and creamy. Stir in a little potato water for even creamier potatoes. Season to taste with salt and pepper.
- Spoon into the prepared baking dish. Dot the top with butter and sprinkle with paprika.
- Bake for 25 minutes until bubbly.

May be prepared ahead and refrigerated after placing in the prepared baking dish. When ready to bake, top with butter and paprika and bake for 30 minutes or until heated through.

Olive Creamed Potatoes

Yield: 5 to 6 servings

2	cups sour cream	1	teaspoon salt
6	medium potatoes, boiled and diced	½	teaspoon pepper
3	tablespoons finely chopped onion	½	teaspoon paprika
2	tablespoons finely chopped pimento-stuffed olives	1	teaspoon chopped parsley

- Spoon sour cream into a skillet. Stir in diced potatoes. Heat slowly over medium heat. When the sour cream begins to bubble over the potatoes, stir in the onion and olives.

- Season with salt and pepper when thoroughly heated. Garnish with paprika and parsley and serve at once.

Decadent Twice Baked Potatoes

Yield: 8 servings

4	large baking potatoes	¾	cup milk, divided
½	cup finely diced Vidalia onion	1	cup shredded extra sharp Cheddar cheese
	Butter or olive oil for sautéing	¾	cup finely grated imported Parmesan cheese
6	strips bacon		
3	tablespoons butter		

- Preheat oven to 450 degrees.

- Wrap potatoes in foil and bake for 1 hour or until done.

- While potatoes bake, sauté onion in butter or olive oil until translucent. Avoid browning. Drain and set aside.

- Fry bacon strips. Drain and cool on a paper towel. When cool, crumble bacon and set aside.

- When potatoes are done, remove them from oven and unwrap from foil. Reduce oven temperature to 350 degrees. Allow potatoes to cool until warm to the touch. While still warm, use a sharp knife to cut potatoes in half lengthwise, being careful not to tear potato skin.

- Gently cut around the inside of the potato halves, leaving ⅛-inch wall of meat on the skin to give skin enough strength to be stuffed.

- Place scooped out potato meat in a large mixing bowl. Add butter and half the milk. Hand mash or whip on low until potatoes are medium stiff, mixing in the rest of the milk, if needed, to make the potatoes desired consistency. Fold in onions, cheeses and half the bacon.

- Stuff potato skins and sprinkle remaining bacon bits over the tops. Place on baking sheet.

- Bake another 20 minutes or until potatoes are hot.

BLACK BEANS AND RICE

Yield: 8 servings

1	(14-ounce) box basmati rice (white or brown)	4	tablespoons finely chopped jalapeño pepper (optional)
1	tablespoon butter or olive oil	1¾	cups finely shredded extra sharp Cheddar or Monterey Jack cheese
1	bunch green onions		
3	(15-ounce) cans black beans	8	ounces sour cream
½	cup roasted peppers, diced		

■ Preheat oven to 325 degrees.

■ Cook rice according to instructions on box. Add butter or olive oil to water. While rice cooks, finely chop the green onions using the white bulbs and the firm green stalks. Set aside.

■ Drain the black beans and reserve the liquid.

■ Place cooked rice in a mixing bowl and fluff with a fork. Mix in onions, roasted pepper and jalapeño, tossing well. Spoon rice mixture into the center of an 8 or 9-inch baking dish, leaving a 1½-inch margin around the sides of the dish.

■ Carefully spoon black beans around the rice. Pour reserved bean liquid over all.

■ Cover rice mixture with cheese and sour cream by spooning 2 tablespoons of each over rice in an intermittent pattern.

■ Cover and bake for approximately 20 minutes.

ARTICHOKES WITH MUSHROOMS

Yield: 4 to 6 servings

¾	pound mushrooms, halved	⅓	cup heavy cream
4	tablespoons butter	½	teaspoon tarragon
2	(8-ounce) packages frozen artichoke hearts		Salt
			Pepper

■ In a saucepan, sauté mushrooms in butter for 5 minutes over medium heat. Stir in frozen artichoke hearts. Cover and simmer 7 to 8 minutes longer. Add the cream and tarragon. Season to taste with salt and pepper.

CHEESY FIESTA RICE

Yield: 6 to 8 servings

1	cup uncooked rice	1	(4-ounce) can jalapeño relish
2	cups chicken broth	½	cup milk
2	tablespoons butter	1	cup sour cream
8	ounces Monterey Jack cheese, cubed	1	cup cottage cheese

■ Preheat oven to 350 degrees.

■ Combine uncooked rice, broth and butter. Mix well. Pour into 2-quart baking dish. Bake, covered, for 40 minutes.

■ In a bowl, combine the cheese cubes, jalapeño relish, milk, sour cream and cottage cheese. Mix well. Fold the cheese mixture into the partially baked rice.

■ Return to the oven and continue baking, uncovered, for 30 minutes.

EASY RICE CASSEROLE

Yield: 6 to 8 servings

1	(10½-ounce) can beef consommé	1	stick butter or margarine
1	(10½-ounce) can French onion soup	1	cup uncooked rice
1	(7-ounce) can sliced mushrooms		

■ Preheat oven to 350 degrees. Lightly grease a 2-quart covered baking dish.

■ Combine the beef consommé, onion soup, mushrooms, butter and rice. Mix well. Pour into prepared baking dish.

■ Bake covered for 1 hour.

This recipe may be cooked in the microwave for 30 minutes. Be sure to stir it once or twice during cooking.

YORKSHIRE PUDDING

Yield: 4 to 6 servings

Hot roast beef drippings	1 cup cold milk
⅞ cup flour	2 eggs
½ teaspoon sugar	

- Preheat oven to 400 degrees.

- Heat a 10 x 10-inch baking dish with ¼ inch of roast beef drippings.

- Blend flour, sugar, milk and eggs until smooth. Keep batter cool.

- Pour cold batter into hot baking dish. Bake at 400 degrees for 20 minutes. Reduce oven temperature to 350 degrees and continue cooking for 10 to 15 minutes more, until fluffy and brown.

- Cut into squares and serve immediately.

This is a delicious accompaniment to a standing rib roast served with au jus gravy and fresh horseradish. It is a wonderful British tradition.

ASPARAGUS BAKED IN WINE SAUCE

Yield: 6 to 8 servings

2 pounds fresh asparagus, cooked	½ teaspoon salt
¼ cup butter	¼ teaspoon pepper
¼ cup white wine	⅓ cup freshly grated Parmesan cheese

- Preheat oven to 425 degrees. Grease an 11 x 7 x 2-inch baking dish.

- Arrange asparagus in the prepared baking dish.

- In a saucepan, melt butter and stir in wine, salt and pepper. Pour over asparagus spears. Sprinkle Parmesan cheese on top.

- Bake uncovered for 15 minutes (25 minutes if dish has been refrigerated).

*B*ROCCOLI *P*ARMESAN

Yield: 4 servings

2	(10-ounce) packages frozen broccoli spears	⅛	teaspoon marjoram
2	tablespoons minced onion	½	teaspoon dry mustard
3	tablespoons butter, melted	1	chicken bouillon cube, crumbled
3	tablespoons flour	2½	cups milk
½	teaspoon salt	¾	cup grated Parmesan cheese, divided
¼	teaspoon pepper		Paprika

- Preheat oven to 375 degrees.

- Cook and drain broccoli. Place in baking dish.

- Sauté onion in butter. Blend in flour, salt, pepper, marjoram and mustard. Cook over medium heat until bubbly. Stir in bouillon cube. Gradually pour in milk. Cook until thick, stirring constantly. Blend in ½ cup Parmesan cheese, stirring until melted.

- Pour sauce over broccoli. Sprinkle with remaining ¼ cup cheese and paprika. Bake 20 to 25 minutes.

*B*ROCCOLI *S*OUFFLÉ

Yield: 4 servings

2	cups chopped broccoli or 1 (10-ounce) package frozen broccoli	½	teaspoon salt
		½	cup milk
2	tablespoons butter	4	eggs, separated
2	tablespoons flour	¼	cup grated Parmesan cheese

- Preheat oven to 350 degrees. Cook and drain broccoli. Do not overcook.

- Melt butter in a medium-sized saucepan and blend in the flour and salt. Add the milk and stir until sauce is bubbling. Remove sauce from heat.

- Beat egg yolks in a 2-cup measuring cup. Slowly stir ½ the hot white sauce into the beaten yolks. Pour yolks and sauce back into the pan of hot white sauce, stirring rapidly.

- Add the cheese and broccoli to the sauce. In a separate bowl, beat the egg whites until stiff peaks form. Fold beaten egg whites into the broccoli mixture. Turn into an ungreased 1-quart soufflé dish. Bake until a knife inserted off-center comes out clean, approximately 35 to 40 minutes. Serve at once.

*H*ORSERADISH *C*ARROTS

Yield: 4 to 6 servings

1	pound carrots	1	tablespoon prepared
½	cup sour cream		horseradish
2	tablespoons chopped onion		

- Slice carrots and boil until tender. Drain off liquid.

- Combine sour cream, onion and horseradish. Pour over the carrots. Serve at once.

*S*WEET *C*ARROTS

Yield: 4 servings

1	pound carrots or baby carrots	1½	tablespoons orange marmalade
1	tablespoon butter		

- Leave baby carrots whole. If using full sized carrots, peel and diagonally cut them into 1½ to 2-inch pieces. Steam carrots until tender.

- Melt butter and marmalade, stirring frequently to prevent sticking and burning. Pour over steamed carrots and toss to coat all pieces. Serve hot.

DILLED CARROTS

Yield: 4 servings

1	pound carrots	½	teaspoon dill weed
1	tablespoon butter, melted	1	teaspoon seasoned salt

■ Cut carrots on the diagonal into 1½ to 2-inch pieces. (Leave baby carrots whole.) Steam until tender.

■ Combine butter, dill weed and seasoned salt. Stir over low heat until salt is dissolved. Pour over carrots to coat well.

EASY EGGPLANT

Yield: 4 servings

1	eggplant, peeled and sliced 1-inch thick	Salt
1	Spanish onion, thickly sliced	Pepper
1-2	tomatoes, in ½-inch thick slices	Butter

■ Preheat oven to 350 degrees.

■ Soak eggplant slices in cold salt water for 30 to 35 minutes. Drain and place in a baking dish. Place onion slices over the eggplant. Put the tomato slices on top of the onion. Season with salt and pepper. Dot with butter.

■ Bake uncovered for 45 minutes.

For food and all thy gifts of love, We give thee thanks and praise. Look down, oh Father, from above And bless us all our days. Amen.

One of the four prayers said by Barbara Principe's daughters.

BAKED EGGPLANT STICKS

Yield: 2 to 4 servings

1   large eggplant
1   tablespoon flour
Salt
Pepper
1   egg beaten

1   cup seasoned breadcrumbs
1   tablespoon sesame seed
1-2 tablespoons vegetable oil

- Preheat oven to 350 degrees. Spread oil in a 9 x 13 x 2-inch baking pan.
- Peel and cut eggplant into sticks (like French fries). Season flour with a little salt and pepper. Roll eggplant sticks in flour, then dip in the egg. Finally, roll each stick in breadcrumbs mixed with sesame seeds.
- Place coated eggplant sticks in prepared baking pan.
- Bake until brown, about 20 to 25 minutes.

EGGPLANT CASSEROLE

Yield: 4 servings

2   eggs, beaten
1   cup milk
¾   teaspoon salt
½   teaspoon sugar
Dash pepper
¼   cup melted butter

1   teaspoon baking powder
1   large eggplant, peeled, cooked and cut in pieces
1   cup breadcrumbs

- Preheat oven to 350 degrees. Grease 1-quart or 8 x 8 x 2-inch baking dish.
- Combine eggs, milk, salt, sugar, pepper, butter and baking powder. Fold in eggplant and breadcrumbs. Mix thoroughly.
- Bake for 30 minutes.

Better a meal of vegetables where there is love than a fattened calf with hatred.

Proverbs 15:17

Sautéed Collard Greens

Yield: 6 servings

2	pounds collard greens	¼	cup chicken broth
6	slices bacon		Salt
1	clove elephant garlic, minced		Freshly ground black pepper

- Wash collards carefully. Remove tough stems. Stack 5 to 6 leaves, roll and thinly slice on the diagonal.

- In a very large skillet, fry the bacon. Crumble bacon after draining on paper towels, and set aside. Reserve grease.

- Stir minced garlic in hot bacon grease but do not allow it to brown. Add the collards and stir to blend garlic and bacon grease with the greens. When collards have wilted, drizzle chicken broth over the greens. Mix, cover and cook over low heat until tender, 15 to 20 minutes. Stir occasionally during cooking.

- Remove from heat and season to taste with salt and pepper. Mix in crumbled bacon and serve hot.

Listen, listen to me, and eat what is good, and your soul will delight in the richest of fare.

Isaiah 55:2

Sautéed Okra

Yield: 6 to 8 servings

2	pounds fresh okra	3	tablespoons butter

- Remove top end of okra and cut crosswise in ½-inch pieces.

- Melt butter in skillet. Cover bottom of skillet with okra. Cook over high heat until okra begins to brown, then turn heat down to medium-high heat. Sauté until brown.

CREOLE GREEN BEANS

Yield: 6 to 8 servings

5 slices bacon	½ teaspoon salt
¾ cup chopped onion	½ teaspoon pepper
½ cup chopped green pepper	1 (14½-ounce) can stewed tomatoes
2 tablespoons flour	1 pound fresh green beans, cooked
2 tablespoons brown sugar	and drained
1 tablespoon Worcestershire sauce	

■ Cook bacon until crisp. Remove bacon from pan and sauté onion and green pepper until tender. Blend in flour, brown sugar, Worcestershire sauce, salt and pepper. Pour in stewed tomatoes and simmer until mixture thickens.

■ Crumble cooked bacon into tomato mixture and stir in green beans. Heat thoroughly.

GARDEN TOUR LUNCHEON MARINATED GREEN BEANS

Yield: 8 servings

1 (16-ounce) package frozen petite whole green beans or 1 pound small fresh green beans	1 (16-ounce) bottle Italian dressing
	¼ cup finely chopped red pepper (optional)

■ Cook beans until tender. Take care not to overcook. Do not salt. Drain cooked beans and rinse in cold water.

■ Pour Italian dressing over beans and stir in red pepper if desired. Mix well.

■ Cover and marinate overnight in refrigerator. Marinated beans will keep up to one week.

Joan Berlin adds 4 ounces crumbled feta cheese or Gorgonzola cheese just before serving.

BAKED BERMUDA ONIONS

Yield: 6 servings

2   large Bermuda onions, peeled and sliced

3   pieces bread, toasted, buttered and cubed

¾   cup shredded cheese

Salt

Black pepper

2   eggs

¾   cup milk

- Preheat oven to 350 degrees. Grease an 8 x 8 x 2-inch baking dish.
- Parboil onions for 15 minutes. Drain onion slices. Arrange layers of onion, toast cubes and cheese in the prepared baking dish, seasoning each layer with salt and pepper.
- Beat eggs and milk. Pour over layered ingredients.
- Bake for 35 minutes in a pan of hot water.

VIDALIA ONION PIE

Yield: 6 to 8 servings

3   cups sliced or cubed Vidalia onions

3   tablespoons butter

1   (9-inch) pie shell

2   eggs, slightly beaten

½   cup evaporated milk

1   teaspoon salt

⅛   teaspoon black pepper

- Preheat oven to 425 degrees.
- Sauté onions in butter until tender. Pour into pastry shell. Combine eggs, milk, salt and pepper. Pour over onions.
- Bake for 18 to 20 minutes, or until golden brown.

Bleu Cheese-Crusted Onions

Yield: 6 servings

2	large Spanish onions, sliced	3	ounces bleu cheese, crumbled
6	tablespoons unsalted butter, at room temperature	2	teaspoons Worcestershire sauce
			Freshly ground black pepper

- Preheat oven to 425 degrees. Position oven rack in center of the oven. Generously butter a 9 x 13 x 2-inch baking dish.

- Spread onion slices evenly in prepared baking dish. In food processor, using knife blade, combine cheese and Worcestershire sauce. Season mixture with black pepper. Spread cheese mixture over sliced onions.

- Bake 20 minutes, then broil briefly until top is brown and bubbly.

Three Pea Stir Fry

Yield: 6 servings

1	tablespoon vegetable oil	6	ounces sugar snap peas, trimmed and cut diagonally into 1-inch pieces
1	large clove garlic, minced		
1	tablespoon peeled and finely chopped fresh ginger	1	cup frozen green peas, unthawed
¼	teaspoon crushed red pepper flakes	1	teaspoon soy sauce
6	ounces snow peas, trimmed and cut diagonally into 1-inch pieces	1	teaspoon Asian sesame oil
		1	tablespoon sesame seeds, toasted

- Heat vegetable oil in a 12-inch nonstick skillet or wok over moderately high heat. Oil should not smoke. Stir fry garlic, ginger and red pepper flakes about 1 minute, until fragrant.

- Add snow peas and sugar snap peas. Stir fry until crisp tender, approximately 3 minutes. Stir in frozen peas and continue cooking 2 minutes more.

- Remove from heat and stir in soy sauce and sesame oil. Sprinkle with toasted sesame seeds and serve.

Broccoli florets may be used with this recipe. If used, place 1 cup in the skillet first. Cook for 1 minute before adding snow peas and snap peas.

*B*LEU *C*HEESE AND *S*PINACH *C*ASSEROLE

Yield: 4 servings

1	(10-ounce) package frozen chopped spinach or 1 (10-ounce) bag fresh spinach	½	cup milk
		¼	cup bleu cheese, crumbled
2	tablespoons butter	3	hard-cooked eggs, peeled and divided
2	tablespoons flour		

- Preheat oven to 350 degrees. Grease a 1-quart casserole dish.

- Cook spinach and drain well.

- Melt butter in a small saucepan and add flour. Pour in milk gradually, stirring constantly. Cook over low heat until thickened. Stir in spinach and crumbled bleu cheese.

- Spoon half the spinach mixture into prepared dish. Slice 1½ eggs over spinach. Repeat with remaining spinach mixture and eggs.

- Cover and bake for 20 minutes.

*S*QUASH AND *A*PPLE *B*AKE

Yield: 6 to 8 servings

½	cup brown sugar	½	cup chopped pecans (optional)
¼	cup melted butter	2	pounds butternut squash, peeled and sliced
½	teaspoon ground mace or nutmeg		
1	tablespoon flour	2-3	Rome or Granny Smith apples, peeled and sliced
½	teaspoon salt		

- Preheat oven to 350 degrees. Grease a 2-quart casserole dish.

- Mix the brown sugar, butter, mace or nutmeg, flour, salt and pecans.

- Layer slices of squash, apples and brown sugar mixture.

- Cover and bake for 1 hour and 15 minutes or until tender.

Squash and Vegetable Medley

Yield: 10 servings

2 medium yellow squash	⅔ cup cider vinegar
3 medium zucchini	¾ cup sugar
½ cup chopped red pepper	1 teaspoon salt
½ cup chopped green onions	1 clove elephant garlic, crushed
½ cup chopped celery	½ teaspoon black pepper
2 tablespoons wine vinegar	⅓ cup vegetable oil

- Wash and slice squash and zucchini into thin rounds. Combine squash, zucchini, red pepper, onions and celery in a large glass bowl and toss well.

- In a saucepan, combine the vinegars, sugar and vegetable oil and bring to a boil. Remove from heat and stir in salt, garlic and pepper.

- Pour marinade over vegetables and stir. Chill at least 12 hours, stirring once or twice. Drain vegetables and serve.

Squash Casserole

Yield: 8 servings

2 tablespoons butter	2 tablespoons juice of fresh lemon
1 medium onion, chopped	8 ounces shredded sharp Cheddar cheese
1½ pounds yellow squash	
1½ pounds zucchini	1 cup sour cream
1 teaspoon salt	1 cup crushed round buttery crackers

- Preheat oven to 350 degrees. Grease a 2½-quart baking dish.

- In a heavy 4-quart saucepan, melt butter and sauté the onion for 10 minutes. Stir to avoid scorching. Combine the squash, zucchini, salt and lemon juice. Cover and cook over medium-low heat. Stir occasionally until enough liquid accumulates to prevent squash from sticking. Simmer until tender, but do not overcook.

- Drain off liquid. Pour squash mixture into prepared baking dish. Stir in cheese, sour cream and crushed crackers. Mix thoroughly.

- Bake uncovered for 30 to 40 minutes.

SQUASH AU GRATIN

Yield: 6 to 8 servings

6	small yellow squash	¾	cup shredded Cheddar cheese, divided
¼	cup chopped onion	¼	cup chopped green pepper
2	tablespoons butter	½	teaspoon salt
2	tablespoons flour	3	tablespoons breadcrumbs
1½	cups milk		Paprika
½	cup liquid from cooked squash		

- Preheat oven to 350 degrees. Grease a 2-quart baking dish.

- Slice squash and cook with the onion in a small amount of water until tender. Drain squash and onions and reserve liquid.

- Melt butter in a saucepan. Add flour and gradually stir in milk and liquid from the squash. Cook, stirring constantly, until sauce is as thick as heavy cream. Season with salt. Combine sauce, ½ cup cheese, green pepper and squash mixture.

- Pour into prepared baking dish. Top with remaining cheese and breadcrumbs. Sprinkle paprika over the top.

- Bake until browned, 20 to 30 minutes.

TOMATO TART

Yield: 8 to 10 servings

	Prepared dough for a 10-inch pie	3	medium ripe tomatoes, peeled and cut into ½-inch slices
2	cups shredded mozzarella cheese	1½	tablespoons olive oil
3	tablespoons chopped fresh basil, divided	¼	teaspoon salt
		¼	teaspoon pepper

- Preheat oven to 400 degrees. Place pie dough in 10-inch tart pan; trim and prick bottom and sides with a fork. Bake for 5 minutes on middle oven rack.

- Sprinkle cheese evenly into shell. Spread 2 tablespoons basil over cheese and arrange tomato slices on top. Brush tomatoes with olive oil. Sprinkle with salt and pepper.

- Place tart pan on a baking sheet. Bake on lowest oven rack for 35 to 40 minutes. Remove and sprinkle remaining basil over tart.

BROILED GARDEN TOMATOES

Yield: 2 servings

2 tomatoes, halved	Sweet basil
Olive oil	Breadcrumbs
Garlic salt	Grated Parmesan cheese

- Preheat boiler.
- Place tomato halves cut side up on a baking sheet lined with aluminum foil.
- Drizzle olive oil over tomatoes, then sprinkle garlic salt, basil, breadcrumbs and cheese.
- Broil for 10 to 15 minutes until browned and tender.

GRILLED VEGETABLE MEDLEY

Yield: 6 servings

Vegetables

1 small eggplant	1 large carrot
1 medium zucchini	1 large red pepper
1 medium yellow squash	1 large red onion

Marinade

2 tablespoons balsamic vinegar (do not substitute)	1 tablespoon chopped fresh basil
2 tablespoons extra-virgin olive oil	½ teaspoon salt
2 tablespoons water	¼ teaspoon freshly ground pepper

- Preheat grill.
- Slice eggplant, zucchini, squash and carrot in ¼-inch diagonal slices. Quarter the red pepper and remove seeds and stem.
- Peel and quarter the onion.
- For marinade, combine balsamic vinegar, olive oil, water, basil, salt and pepper. Mix thoroughly.
- Brush both sides of vegetables with marinade or place vegetables in a plastic bag with marinade to coat them.
- Alternate vegetables on 8-inch wooden skewers.
- Grill about 6 to 10 minutes, until vegetables are tender and show grill marks. Turn once during grilling.

Zucchini in Alfredo Sauce

Yield: 8 servings

5 large zucchini (about 2½ pounds)	⅔ cup light cream
1 teaspoon salt	½ cup finely grated Parmesan cheese
2 tablespoons olive oil	plus some for topping
2-3 cloves garlic, minced	Coarsely ground black pepper
1 (8-ounce) package cream cheese, cubed and softened	Ground nutmeg

- Cut zucchini into ¼-inch thick strips. Place in a colander and toss with salt. Allow to sit and drain for 1 hour. Rinse, drain again and pat dry.

- Heat olive oil in a 12-inch skillet. Cook zucchini with minced garlic for 2 to 4 minutes until crisp and tender. Transfer to a large bowl.

- In the same skillet, heat cream cheese and cream over medium-low heat until it is smooth, stirring often. Pour in ½ cup Parmesan cheese and mix well. Return the zucchini to the pan and heat thoroughly. Season to taste with pepper and nutmeg. Sprinkle Parmesan cheese over the top.

Corn-Zucchini Casserole

Yield: 6 servings

1 pound zucchini, cut into ½-inch slices	1 cup shredded Swiss cheese
¼ cup chopped onion	½ teaspoon salt
2 tablespoons butter, divided	¼ cup breadcrumbs
2 cups corn, cooked	2 tablespoons grated Parmesan cheese
2 eggs, beaten	

- Preheat oven to 350 degrees. Grease a 1-quart baking dish.

- Cook and mash zucchini. Sauté onion in 1 tablespoon butter until tender. Combine corn, zucchini, onion, eggs, Swiss cheese and salt. Mix well and pour mixture into prepared baking dish.

- Mix breadcrumbs and Parmesan cheese. Melt remaining tablespoon butter. Combine butter with crumbs and cheese. Sprinkle mixture on top of casserole.

- Bake for 40 minutes.

*I*TALIAN-*S*TYLE *Z*UCCHINI

Yield: 6 servings

1½ pounds zucchini, sliced
½ cup chopped onion
4 tablespoons butter
1 egg, beaten
½ teaspoon poppy seed

½ teaspoon minced garlic
¼ teaspoon salt
Dash pepper
Parmesan cheese

■ Preheat oven to 375 degrees.

■ Sauté zucchini and onion in butter. Stir in egg, poppy seed, garlic, salt and pepper. Gently mix and spoon into a 1½-quart baking dish. Sprinkle Parmesan cheese over the top.

■ Bake for 30 minutes.

*Z*UCCHINI OR *E*GGPLANT *C*ASSEROLE

Yield: 6 servings

2 pounds zucchini or eggplant, sliced
1½ tablespoons butter
½ cup sour cream
4 tablespoons shredded sharp
    Cheddar cheese
½ teaspoon salt

⅛ teaspoon paprika
1 egg yolk, beaten
1 tablespoon chopped chives
1 tablespoon chopped green onion
Breadcrumbs

■ Preheat oven to 350 degrees.

■ Boil zucchini or eggplant until just tender. Drain and place in a 1½-quart baking dish. In a saucepan, melt the butter. Stir sour cream, shredded cheese, salt and paprika into the butter. Once the cheese has melted, add the egg yolk, chives and green onion.

■ Pour cheese mixture over zucchini or eggplant slices, gently mixing. Sprinkle with breadcrumbs.

■ Bake for 20 minutes.

Vegetables & Accompaniments

"Summer Bounty"
by Libby Bennett

Condiments & Sauces

Condiments & Sauces

WATERMELON RIND PICKLE

Yield: 9 to 12 pints

7	pounds watermelon rind	2	tablespoons allspice
2	tablespoons pickling lime per gallon of water		Lemon slices, as desired
	Water to cover rinds		Dried ginger, as desired
2	tablespoons whole cloves	6	pounds sugar
1	cinnamon stick	2	cups water, heated
		1	quart vinegar

- Peel and cut rinds into finger-length strips. Be sure to remove all the pink from the rinds. Soak rinds overnight in water and pickling lime. Drain. Rinse rinds well and cover with ice water. Let stand until well chilled. Drain.

- Cook in clear water for 20 minutes. Drain.

- Tie cloves, cinnamon and allspice in a gauze bag. Include lemon and ginger, if desired.

- Mix the sugar, hot water and vinegar. Bring to a boil and add the gauze bag with spices. Drain the watermelon rind and add to the mixture. Simmer uncovered until the watermelon rind is transparent and can be easily pierced with a toothpick, about 45 to 60 minutes.

- Sterilize jars in boiling water for 5 minutes or wash in the dishwasher. The top inserts must be new.

- Spoon the rind into hot sterilized jars, cover with the hot syrup. Seal the jars.

SWEET CUCUMBER PICKLES

Yield: 9 to 12 pints

1	cup pickling lime	½	gallon cider vinegar
2	gallons water	2	sticks cinnamon
7	pounds pickling cucumbers		Handful pickling spices
4⅓	pounds sugar	2	tablespoons salt

- Add pickling lime to water and stir well. Slice cucumbers ¼-inch thick. Soak cucumbers in the limewater for 24 hours, stirring occasionally. Rinse well and drain.

- Combine sugar, vinegar, cinnamon and pickling spices. Let cucumbers stand in this mixture for 24 hours. Bring this to a boil; add salt to the brine when boiling point is reached. Boil cucumbers for 20 minutes.

- Pack into pint sterile jars and seal.

CRANBERRY RELISH

Yield: 2 cups

2	oranges	1	pound fresh cranberries
1	lemon	2	cups sugar

- Seed and cut up orange and lemon.
- Chop the fruit in a blender or food processor, starting with half the citrus fruit, then half the cranberries.
- Mix fruit and sugar.
- Refrigerate up to 3 weeks or freeze.

Mix this in small batches.

FIG CHUTNEY

Yield: 4 to 5 half-pint jars

2	pounds fresh figs, trimmed and quartered	1	tablespoon slivered crystallized ginger
1	cup raisins	9	whole cloves
1	cup red wine vinegar	1	tablespoon balsamic vinegar
¾	cup honey	½	tablespoon mustard seeds

- Combine the figs, raisins, wine vinegar, honey, ginger, cloves, balsamic vinegar and mustard seeds in a non-aluminum pot. Bring to a boil. Reduce heat, cover and simmer for 15 minutes until figs are tender.
- Store in sterile jars. Chutney may be stored in an airtight container in refrigerator for up to 2 weeks. Serve with pork, curry or over cream cheese as an appetizer.

This recipe may be made in batches up to four times as large.

GARDEN TOUR LUNCHEON SPICED PEACHES

Yield: 10 to 14 servings

2	(29-ounce) cans peach halves	1	cup white cider vinegar
1⅓	cups sugar	4	cinnamon sticks
		2	teaspoons whole cloves

- Drain peach juice into a large saucepan. Add the sugar and vinegar.
- Tie cinnamon sticks and cloves in a bouquet garni and place in the liquid. Rapidly boil for 10 minutes.
- Pour the hot liquid over the peaches and refrigerate overnight. This will keep in the refrigerator for several days.

THE POMEGRANITE

LEMON CURD

Yield: 1 cup

	Rind of 1 lemon	1	cup sugar
1	stick butter	½	cup juice of fresh lemons
3	egg whites, stiffly beaten		Pinch of salt

- Combine the lemon rind, butter, beaten egg whites, sugar, lemon juice and salt. Cook in top of a double boiler until thick. Refrigerate. Serve over ladyfingers or pound cake.

Jim's Favorite Barbecue Sauce

Yield: 5 cups

Hardy Robinson fondly recalls a Blackstone, Virginia friend using this sauce for his famous barbecued chicken. He cooked the chicken on chicken wire over a pit, basting it often with the sauce. This sauce is also delicious with pork.

1	pint tomato juice	½	teaspoon pepper
2	tablespoons lemon juice	½	teaspoon salt
1	cup ketchup	1	tablespoon chili powder
½	teaspoon sugar	1	tablespoon dry mustard
½	cup vinegar	1	bay leaf
2	tablespoons steak sauce	1½	tablespoons celery seed
1½	tablespoons Worcestershire sauce		

- Bring tomato juice, lemon juice, ketchup, sugar, vinegar, steak sauce, Worcestershire sauce, pepper, salt, chili powder, dry mustard and bay leaf to a boil. Turn heat down and simmer sauce for 1½ hours.

- In another small pan boil the celery seed for a few minutes and strain off the water. Add seeds to sauce.

Marvelous Marinade

Yield: 1¼ cups

1	cup water	1	tablespoon sugar
¼	cup light soy sauce	¼	teaspoon ground ginger
2-4	cloves garlic, minced		

- Combine water, soy sauce, garlic, sugar and ginger.

- Seal marinade in plastic bag with 2 pounds of beef, pork or chicken. Marinate for several hours.

Condiments & Sauces

*E*ASY *S*AUCE FOR *B*ERRIES

Yield: ¾ cup

½ cup whipping cream   3 ounces white chocolate

- Heat cream to near boil. Add chocolate and cook until melted, being careful not to boil.
- Serve over strawberries or blueberries.

*S*WEET OR *S*AVORY *F*RUITY *S*ALSA

Yield: 3 cups

1 pint strawberries, hulled and coarsely chopped	2 tablespoons juice of fresh limes
1 cup coarsely chopped fresh pineapple (for sweet) or avocado (for savory)	2 tablespoons honey
	½ teaspoon grated fresh ginger (for sweet) or 1-2 tablespoons seeded and finely chopped jalapeño pepper (for savory)
½ cup coarsely chopped mango or peach (for sweet) or cucumber (for savory)	
1 teaspoon finely grated lime peel	¼ teaspoon cracked black pepper

- For sweet salsa, combine strawberries, pineapple, mango or peach, lime peel, lime juice, honey, ginger and cracked black pepper.
- For savory salsa, combine strawberries, avocado, cucumber, lime peel, lime juice, honey, jalapeño pepper and cracked black pepper.
- Cover and chill 2 to 24 hours.

MINT SAUCE

Yield: ¾ cup

This New Zealand recipe from Cheryl Jordan's mother will keep in the refrigerator for weeks.

¼ cup boiling water
1 tablespoon sugar

¼ cup finely chopped mint leaves
½ cup cider vinegar

- Pour boiling water over sugar and mint leaves. Stir and add vinegar.

- Serve at room temperature with roast lamb or lamb chops in lieu of mint jelly.

MARINARA SAUCE

Yield: 6 servings

6 (14½-ounce) cans stewed tomatoes with onions, celery and green peppers
12 cloves garlic, finely chopped

12 pieces flat or round anchovies
2 tablespoons virgin olive oil
2 tablespoons dry Italian seasoning

- In a blender, process stewed tomatoes to desired coarseness. Sauté garlic and anchovy pieces in olive oil. Add Italian seasoning by rolling or pressing it between fingers.

- When anchovies have "melted," add tomatoes. Simmer to almost boiling for at least 60 minutes. Refrigerate overnight so flavors can marry.

FRUIT TOPPING

Yield: 4 servings

⅔ cup sour cream (may use reduced-fat)

⅓ cup brown sugar

- Blend sour cream and brown sugar until sugar dissolves.

- Use approximately ⅔ sour cream to ⅓ brown sugar or to taste.

Poppy Seed Dressing

Yield: Approximately 3 cups

1	cup sugar	3	tablespoons onion juice
2	teaspoons dry mustard	2	cups vegetable oil
2	teaspoons salt	3	tablespoons poppy seeds
⅔	cup vinegar		

- Combine sugar, mustard and salt. Stir in the vinegar and onion juice, mixing thoroughly.

- Slowly pour in oil, beating constantly. Continue beating until dressing is thick. Add poppy seeds and beat for 2 or 3 more minutes. Refrigerate.

Arthur Family Mayonnaise

Yield: 1½ cups

1	teaspoon salt	1	cup olive oil
1	teaspoon paprika	1	tablespoon juice of fresh lemon
1	teaspoon dry mustard		
2	egg yolks	1	tablespoon tarragon vinegar
1	tablespoon boiling water		

- Mix salt, paprika and mustard in a small mixer bowl. Add egg yolks and water. Beat well.

- Slowly add olive oil and continue beating until mixture reaches proper consistency.

- Once mixture reaches desired consistency, beat in lemon juice and vinegar.

This recipe may be made in blender as well.

White House Salad Dressing

Yield: 4 cups

1	pint real mayonnaise	Salt and pepper to taste	
3-4	ounces bleu cheese, finely crumbled	1	teaspoon garlic powder
		1-1¼	cups buttermilk

- Combine the mayonnaise and bleu cheese. Add salt and pepper to taste, then add garlic powder.

- Stir in buttermilk until dressing reaches desired consistency and refrigerate. Stir well before serving.

It is important to refrigerate this dressing for several days in order to allow the flavors to marry.

Herb and Garlic Salad Dressing

Yield: 1½ cups

1	cup vegetable oil	½	teaspoon salt
½	cup cider vinegar	2	teaspoons minced garlic
⅛	teaspoon crushed red pepper	1	teaspoon dried oregano
½	teaspoon paprika	½	teaspoon dried thyme
½	teaspoon seasoned garlic salt		

- Combine the oil, vinegar, red pepper, paprika, garlic salt, salt, garlic, oregano and thyme.

- Blend or mix by shaking well. Cover and refrigerate.

"Avignon Alfresco"
by William Campbell

Desserts

Desserts

Blueberry Tart Royale

Yield: 5 servings

Pie crust pastry
3   tablespoons cornstarch
4   tablespoons water
4   cups blueberries, divided
3   tablespoons sugar

Juice of ¼ lemon
Grated rind of ¼ lemon
4   ounces raspberry liqueur, divided
Sweetened whipped cream, as topping

■ Preheat oven to 375 degrees. Grease a 9-inch pie pan.

■ Line the pie pan with the pie crust and cover it with foil, shiny side down. Spread weights (dry beans or rice) over the foil to hold pastry in place and bake for 10 minutes. Remove the weights and foil and continue baking until done, about 20 minutes. Cool pastry.

■ Mix the cornstarch and water. Combine 1 cup of berries, sugar, lemon juice, lemon zest, 2 ounces raspberry liqueur and cornstarch mixture in a medium-sized saucepan. Bring to a boil over medium heat, stirring often. Cook, continuing to stir, for 10 minutes more. The mixture will thicken to the consistency of jam. Add the remaining berries and liqueur. Stir for about 1 minute and pour into the pre-cooked pie crust. Smooth the top. Serve either warm or chilled with whipped cream.

Easy Pecan Pie

Yield: 8 servings

1   pie crust
1   pound light brown sugar
1   stick butter, softened

3   eggs, beaten
2   teaspoons vanilla extract
1-1½ cups pecan pieces

■ Preheat oven to 350 degrees. Bake pie crust for 5 minutes.

■ Blend sugar and butter. Microwave mixture for 2½ minutes.

■ Thoroughly mix eggs and vanilla into the mixture. Pour into precooked pie crust. Sprinkle top with pecan pieces.

■ Bake 45 to 50 minutes.

Macaroon Pie

Yield: 6 to 8 servings

3 egg whites, beaten stiff
Pinch of salt
1 teaspoon baking powder
6 saltines, finely rolled or crushed

1 cup sugar plus 2 tablespoons, divided
½ cup finely chopped pecans
1½ teaspoons vanilla, divided
1 cup heavy cream

■ Preheat oven to 300 degrees. Grease and flour a 9-inch pie pan.

■ Beat the egg whites with a pinch of salt until stiff peaks form. Fold in the baking powder, saltines, 1 cup sugar, pecans and 1 teaspoon vanilla. Spoon the mixture over the bottom and sides of the pie pan. Bake for 40 minutes. Remove from the oven and cool completely.

■ Whip the cream with 2 tablespoons of sugar and ½ teaspoon vanilla until stiff peaks form. Spread the whipped cream over the top of the pie. Chill for 20 minutes before serving.

Beth's Strawberry Pie

Yield: 6 to 8 servings

1 deep-dish pie shell, baked and cooled
1 quart strawberries, washed, capped and divided
1 cup sugar

3 tablespoons cornstarch
1 cup water
4 tablespoons strawberry flavored gelatin
Red food coloring if desired

■ Bake prepared pie shell according to directions and cool.

■ Cover the bottom of the pie shell with whole, upright strawberries. Dice the remaining berries and set aside. Combine the sugar and cornstarch in a saucepan and add water gradually. Cook over medium heat, stirring to prevent sticking, until mixture is thick.

■ Remove from heat and add the strawberry flavored gelatin and food coloring. Stir until the flavored gelatin is dissolved. Add the diced strawberries to the hot syrup. Blend and pour over the whole berries. Refrigerate until set.

Lemon Chess Pie

Yield: 12 to 16 servings

½ cup butter
2 cups sugar
5 eggs
1 cup milk
1 tablespoon flour

1 tablespoon white or yellow cornmeal
Juice of 2 lemons
Grated peel of 2 lemons
2 (9-inch) uncooked pie shells

■ Preheat oven to 350 degrees.

■ Blend the butter and sugar. Add eggs, milk, flour, cornmeal, lemon juice and lemon rind.

■ Fill the pie shells and bake for 30 to 40 minutes. Cool and serve.

Apple Dumplings

Yield: 4 servings

2 crisp, tart apples (Granny Smith)
Juice of ½ lemon
1 cup sugar plus 2-3 tablespoons, divided
Cinnamon to taste
Nutmeg to taste

1 cup water
⅛ teaspoon cinnamon
⅛ teaspoon nutmeg
4 tablespoons butter, divided
1 (9-inch) frozen pie shell, thawed

■ Preheat oven to 375 degrees. Grease a 9 x 9 x 2-inch baking dish.

■ Peel and core the apples, cutting them into small pieces. Squeeze lemon juice over the apples and stir them to coat. Liberally sprinkle sugar, cinnamon and nutmeg over the apples.

■ Combine 1 cup sugar, water, ⅛ teaspoon cinnamon and ⅛ teaspoon nutmeg in a saucepan. Bring to a boil and cook for 5 minutes. Add 2 tablespoons butter and set aside.

■ Roll pie crust pastry between two sheets of waxed paper to thin and enlarge it. Cut the pastry into 4 equal pieces. Spoon a mound of apples onto each piece and dot with remaining butter. Fold the corners of each pastry into the center and pinch the edges to seal the dumplings.

■ Place the dumplings 1-inch apart in the baking dish. Pour the syrup over the dumplings. Lightly sprinkle sugar and cinnamon over the top. Bake for 35 minutes. Serve dumplings warm with rum or brandy-flavored hard sauce or vanilla ice cream.

Maude's Sweet Potato Pie

Yield: 6 servings

1	cup cooked and mashed sweet potato	2	tablespoons butter, melted
2	eggs, beaten	1	teaspoon vanilla extract
½	cup sugar	½	teaspoon cinnamon
¼	cup evaporated milk	1	(9-inch) uncooked pie shell

■ Preheat oven to 350 degrees.

■ Combine the sweet potato, eggs and sugar. Beat well. Add the evaporated milk, melted butter, vanilla and cinnamon. Stir until well blended.

■ Pour mixture into the pie shell and bake for about 1 hour or until knife inserted in the center comes out clean.

Lemon Zest Pie

Yield: 6 to 8 servings

2	tablespoons milk	4	eggs
1	lemon, seeded and cut into small pieces	1	stick butter or margarine, melted
	Juice of 1 lemon	2	cups sugar
		1	(9-inch) deep dish pie shell

■ Preheat oven to 350 degrees.

■ Combine the milk, lemon pieces, lemon juice, eggs, butter and sugar in the blender. Blend until mixture is smooth.

■ Pour into pie shell and bake for 30 minutes or until firm in the middle. Cool and serve.

If a regular pie shell is used instead of a deep-dish one, there will be enough filling left over to fill an ovenproof custard cup, for tasting.

EASY LIGHT PUMPKIN MOUSSE PIE

Yield: 6 to 8 servings

1	(4-ounce) package vanilla pudding mix	1	graham cracker pie crust
¾	cup cold milk	1	(8-ounce) container frozen whipped topping, thawed and divided
½	cup canned pumpkin		
¾	teaspoon pumpkin pie spice		

◼ Combine the dry pudding mix and cold milk. Mix well and blend in the pumpkin and the pumpkin pie spice. Fold in 2 cups of whipped topping.

◼ Spoon the mixture into the pie shell and refrigerate for at least 4 hours. Cover with remaining whipped topping before serving.

COCONUT PIE

BELVEDERE

Yield: 12 to 16 servings

2	(1.3-ounce) packages whipped topping mix	1	teaspoon vanilla extract
1	pint heavy cream	½	cup sour cream
2	(3-ounce) packages instant coconut pudding mix	1	cup frozen or fresh coconut
1½-2	cups milk	2	prepared cookie or graham cracker pie crusts

◼ On high speed, beat whipped topping mix and heavy cream until thick. Add both packages instant pudding mix, milk and vanilla. Beat on low speed. Mix in sour cream. Fold in coconut and mix.

◼ Pour mixture into prepared pie shells and refrigerate at least 6 to 8 hours or, preferably, overnight.

Mummee's Fruit Dumplings with Sherry Hard Sauce

Yield: 8 to 10 servings

Dumplings

1	(15-ounce) package refrigerated pie crust dough
2	quarts blackberries

2	tablespoons sugar or more to taste
1/16	teaspoon cinnamon
1/2	stick butter, cut in 1/8-inch slices

Sherry Hard Sauce

1/3	teaspoon butter, softened
1	egg yolk

2 1/2	cups confectioners' sugar
2	tablespoons sherry

- Preheat oven to 450 degrees. Grease an 11 x 9-inch baking pan or two 9-inch pie plates.
- Cut each round of pie crust dough into 4 sections. Place 1/2 cup of fruit on each section. Sprinkle fruit with sugar and cinnamon. Dot each with a 1/8-inch pat of butter.
- Fold dough around the fruit and place in the prepared pan or pie plates. Bake for 15 minutes at 450 degrees. Reduce oven temperature to 350 degrees and bake 30 minutes more.
- For the hard sauce, combine butter, egg yolk, sugar and sherry in a blender. Blend thoroughly.
- Refrigerate until firm. Spoon over hot fruit dumplings.

1 quart of blueberries, 2 quarts of cherries or 8 sliced peaches may be substituted for the blackberries.

Gran's Lemon Chiffon Pie

Yield: 6 to 8 servings

1	precooked (9-inch) pie shell
4	eggs, separated
1 1/4	cups sugar, divided

1	teaspoon grated lemon peel
1/4	cup lemon juice
	Dash salt

- Preheat oven to 325 degrees.
- In a double boiler, cook egg yolks with 3/4 cup sugar, lemon peel and lemon juice, stirring until thickened.
- Beat egg whites with salt until stiff but not dry. Slowly beat in 1/2 cup sugar. Fold into hot lemon mixture.
- Spoon into precooked pie shell and bake 15 to 20 minutes or until golden. Cool. Pie filling will settle a bit.

*B*LUEBERRY *C*RISP

Yield: 6 to 8 servings

4	cups fresh blueberries	½	teaspoon cinnamon
1	teaspoon grated lemon rind	¼	teaspoon nutmeg (if desired)
¼	cup sugar (as needed)	¼	cup butter, softened
½	cup flour	½	cup brown sugar
½	cup rolled oats		

- Preheat oven to 375 degrees and grease an 8 x 8 x 2-inch pan.

- Wash and drain blueberries. Cover the bottom of the greased pan with the berries. Sprinkle berries with lemon rind and sugar.

- In a separate bowl blend the flour, oats, cinnamon, nutmeg, butter and brown sugar. Drop this mixture over the berries.

- Bake for 30 minutes or until topping is golden. Serve warm either plain or with cream.

*K*itty Crittenden created this recipe to reproduce "Blueberry Fundy," from childhood memories of summers spent on Cape Forchu, Yarmouth, Nova Scotia, Canada, an island situated at the mouth of the Bay of Fundy.

*P*EACH *C*OBBLER

Yield: 6 to 8 servings

3	cups sliced peaches	1	egg, beaten
1	cup flour		Dash cinnamon or nutmeg
1	cup sugar	6	tablespoons butter, melted

- Preheat oven to 350 degrees.

- Place sliced peaches in a greased 9 x 9 x 2-inch baking dish. Combine the flour and sugar. Add the egg to the dry mixture and mix with a fork until crumbly. Spread this over the peaches.

- Drizzle the melted butter over the crumb topping. Bake for 35 minutes.

Angel Pie

Yield: 8 servings

Meringue Crust

3 egg whites	1 teaspoon vanilla
½ teaspoon baking powder	1 teaspoon vinegar
⅛ teaspoon salt	1 teaspoon water
1 cup sugar	

Filling

4 egg yolks, beaten	2 tablespoons grated lemon rind
½ cup sugar	1½ cups whipping cream
2 tablespoons lemon juice, or juice of 3 lemons	Sugar to taste

- Preheat the oven to 275 degrees. Grease a 9-inch pie pan.

- Beat the egg whites, baking powder and salt with an electric mixer at high speed until very stiff. While mixing, add the sugar a spoonful at a time.

- Mix the vanilla, vinegar and water and add to the egg white mixture.

- Pour this into the pie pan and bake for 1 hour. Cool.

- For filling, beat the yolks, add sugar and beat again. Add lemon juice and rind.

- In a double boiler, cook until quite thick. Cool.

- Whip the cream, adding sugar to taste. Spread half of this whipped cream over the meringue.

- Add the lemon filling. Spread the remainder of the whipped cream on top of the filling. Refrigerate overnight.

Easy Key Lime Pie

Yield: 6 to 8 servings

1 baked pie shell	4 ounces frozen nondairy whipped topping
1 (14-ounce) can condensed milk	
¼ cup key lime juice	

- Combine the condensed milk and lime juice and pour into baked pie shell.

- Refrigerate at least 2 hours. Before serving, top with frozen nondairy whipped topping.

CRANBERRY-WALNUT TART

Yield: 8 to 10 servings

Basic Pastry

1¾ cups all-purpose flour
½ teaspoon salt
½ cup plus 1 tablespoon butter

3 tablespoons vegetable shortening, cut into pieces
3-5 tablespoons ice water

Filling

1 (12-ounce) package cranberries
½ cup packed light brown sugar
1 tablespoon grated orange rind
½ cup fresh orange juice

4 tablespoons butter
¼ teaspoon ground cinnamon
¼ teaspoon ground ginger
¾ cup walnut pieces

- For pastry, combine flour, salt, butter, shortening and ice water. Blend well. Chill pastry dough for 1 hour before rolling out.
- On a lightly floured board, roll dough into a 12-inch circle, ⅛-inch thick. Carefully line a 10-inch tart pan. Refrigerate while preparing filling.
- Preheat oven to 350 degrees.
- Simmer cranberries, sugar, orange rind and orange juice over medium heat until thickened. Remove from heat and stir in butter, cinnamon and ginger. Let cool and add walnut pieces.
- Fill pastry with cool cranberry mixture. Bake for 30 to 40 minutes until crust is golden brown and filling is just bubbling.

CHOCOLATE SILK PIE

MILLER & RHOADS

Yield: 6 to 8 slices

1 (9-inch) frozen pie crust, thawed
1 stick butter
¾ cup sugar
1 teaspoon vanilla

3 squares unsweetened chocolate, divided
2 eggs
1 cup whipped cream

- Bake the thawed pie crust for 6 to 9 minutes until slightly brown. Put aside to cool.
- Beat butter and sugar with vanilla and put aside.
- Melt 2 squares of the chocolate in a double boiler. Let the mixture cool and thicken. Do not allow it to harden. Add the butter and sugar mixture to the chocolate and beat thoroughly.
- Add 1 egg and beat for 5 minutes. Add the second egg and again beat for 5 minutes.
- Pour the mixture into the pie crust and refrigerate until cool. Spread whipped cream on top. Grate remaining square of chocolate. Dust grated chocolate over pie.

STRAWBERRY SATIN PIE

Yield: 6 to 8 slices

Pie

1	(9-inch) frozen pie crust, thawed	2	cups milk
½	cup sliced toasted almonds	1	egg, slightly beaten
½	cup sugar	1	teaspoon vanilla
3	tablespoons cornstarch	½	cup whipped cream
3	tablespoons all-purpose flour	2½	cups strawberries, halved
½	teaspoon salt		

Glaze

½	cup strawberries, mashed	2	teaspoons cornstarch
½	cup of water	5-10	drops of red food coloring
¼	cup of sugar		

- Preheat oven to 400 degrees.

- Bake the thawed pie crust for 6 to 9 minutes until crust is slightly brown. Spread almonds over the crust. Set aside to cool.

- Combine sugar, cornstarch, flour and salt in a double boiler.

- Heat and gradually add the milk to the mixture. Stir until thick. Add a little of the hot mixture to the slightly beaten egg and mix rapidly. Add the vanilla.

- Add the egg mixture to the cream mixture in the double boiler. Heat until just beginning to boil. Set aside to cool and then chill in the refrigerator.

- When chilled, beat well and fold in whipped cream. Pour the mixture into the baked pie crust. Arrange the sliced berries on top saving a few to put on top of the glaze.

- For the glaze, put the mashed berries in a double boiler. Add the water and cook 2 minutes. Sieve and return berry juice to the double boiler.

- Mix the sugar and cornstarch with the berry juice in the double boiler. Add red food coloring. Stir until thick and clear. Cool.

- Pour glaze over the strawberries. Decorate with the reserved slices. Refrigerate until serving time. A dab of whipped cream can be added on each slice.

Desserts—Pies and Cobblers

CARROT CAKE

Yield: 18 to 24 servings

Cake

2	cups sugar	2	teaspoons cinnamon
4	eggs	½	teaspoon salt
2	cups all-purpose flour, sifted	1	teaspoon vanilla extract
2	teaspoons baking powder	1¼	cups vegetable oil
2	teaspoons baking soda	3	cups grated carrots
		½-1	cup chopped pecans

Frosting

1	(3-ounce) package cream cheese, softened	3	cups sifted confectioners' sugar
½	cup butter, softened	1	teaspoon vanilla extract

- Preheat oven to 350 degrees. Grease and flour a 9 x 13 x 2-inch baking pan.

- Blend sugar and eggs. Sift flour, baking powder, baking soda, cinnamon and salt. Mix vanilla and oil with sifted ingredients. Combine with egg mixture and mix well. Stir in carrots and pecans. Spoon batter into prepared pan.

- Bake for 45 to 50 minutes.

- For frosting, blend cream cheese and butter. Gradually beat in confectioners' sugar and vanilla extract.

- Spread on cool cake.

May the favor of the Lord our God rest upon us; establish the work of our hands for us— yes, establish the work of our hands.

Psalm 90:17

Apple Cake

Yield: 12 to 16 servings

Cake

3	eggs	1	teaspoon baking soda
1¼	cups vegetable oil	2	teaspoons baking powder
2	cups sugar	1	teaspoon nutmeg
2½	cups all-purpose flour	2	dashes allspice
1	teaspoon salt	3	cups peeled and diced apples

Frosting

1	stick butter, softened	Confectioners' sugar
1	(8-ounce) package cream cheese, softened	Nutmeg
		Pecan pieces

- Preheat oven to 350 degrees. Spray a 10-inch fluted tube pan with cooking spray.

- Combine eggs, oil and sugar. Sift flour, salt, baking soda, baking powder, nutmeg and allspice. Gradually stir sifted ingredients into sugar mixture. Mix thoroughly. Fold in apples and turn into prepared pan.

- Bake 1 hour.

- For frosting, combine butter, cream cheese and enough sugar for mixture to have desired consistency and sweetness.

- Spread over cake. Grate nutmeg and sprinkle nutmeg and pecans over top.

Enter his gates with thanksgiving and his courts with praise; give thanks to him and praise his name.

Psalm 100:4

Desserts—Cakes

$\mathcal{T}$IPSY $\mathcal{C}$AKE

Yield: 10 to 12 servings

1	quart whole milk	2	(3-ounce) packages split ladyfingers
1	cup sugar		Sweet cream sherry
4	eggs, well beaten	½	pint heavy cream
1	(14-ounce) can condensed milk	1	(6-ounce) package sliced almonds

■ In a medium saucepan combine milk, sugar, eggs and condensed milk. Cook over low to medium heat, stirring constantly until it thickens and coats a spoon. Do not boil. Final temperature of custard should be no more than 180 degrees. Cool and refrigerate in covered container.

■ Layer split ladyfingers in a 9 x 13 x 2-inch baking dish. Sprinkle generously with cream sherry or to taste. Cover lady fingers with custard and add a second layer of lady fingers. Again sprinkle sherry over ladyfingers and cover with custard.

■ Keep covered and refrigerated until ready to serve. Toast the almonds gently in a 250-degree oven. Top each serving with a dollop of whipped cream and sprinkle with toasted almonds.

$\mathcal{M}$EXICAN $\mathcal{F}$RUIT $\mathcal{C}$AKE

Yield: 2 full loaves or 4 mini-loaves

1	cup sugar (scant)	3-4	cups walnuts
1½	cups all-purpose flour	4	cups pecans
2	teaspoons baking powder	5-6	eggs, separated
2	pounds chopped dates	1½	cups whisky
1	pound candied cherries	1	tablespoon vanilla extract
1	pound candied pineapple		

■ Preheat oven to 250 degrees. Grease two 9 x 5 x 3-inch loaf pans or four 4½ x 2¾ x 1¼-inch loaf pans.

■ Mix sugar, flour and baking powder. Sift over dates, cherries, pineapple, walnuts and pecans.

■ Beat egg yolks. Add to dry ingredients and fruit. Pour in whiskey and vanilla. Mix well. Beat egg whites and fold into fruit mixture.

■ Spoon batter into prepared loaf pans. Bake 2 hours. Cool. Wrap tightly in foil.

Cakes will keep for at least 1 month unfrozen.

NORVELL'S CHOCOLATE POUND CAKE

Yield: 16 to 20 servings

2 sticks butter or margarine	1 teaspoon salt
½ cup shortening	½ teaspoon baking powder
3 cups sugar	½ cup cocoa
5 eggs	2 cups milk
3 cups all-purpose flour	2 teaspoons vanilla

■ Preheat oven to 315 degrees. Grease a 9 or 10-inch tube pan.

■ Blend butter, shortening and sugar in a large bowl. Add eggs one at a time, beating after each addition.

■ Combine flour, salt, baking powder and cocoa and sift together twice.

■ Add milk and vanilla alternately with sifted ingredients to the butter mixture, ending with milk.

■ Pour batter into prepared tube pan. Bake for 80 minutes.

HOT MILK POUND CAKE

Yield: 12 to 16 servings

6 eggs	3 cups all-purpose flour, sifted
3 cups sugar	1½ teaspoons vanilla extract
2 sticks butter or margarine	2¼ teaspoons baking powder
1½ cups hot milk	

■ Preheat oven to 350 degrees. Grease and flour a 9 or 10-inch tube pan.

■ Beat eggs and sugar.

■ Melt butter in hot milk. Pour into egg mixture, alternating milk and sifted flour. Beat in vanilla and baking powder.

■ Pour batter into prepared tube pan. Bake for 45 minutes.

Five Flavor Pound Cake

Yield: 16 servings

Cake

3	cups sugar	1	cup milk
2	sticks butter	1	teaspoon rum extract
½	cup shortening	1	teaspoon butter extract
5	eggs	1	teaspoon vanilla extract
3	cups all-purpose flour	1	teaspoon coconut extract
1	teaspoon baking powder	1	teaspoon lemon extract

Glaze

¼	cup water	½	teaspoon vanilla extract
½	cup sugar	½	teaspoon coconut extract
½	teaspoon rum extract	½	teaspoon lemon extract
½	teaspoon butter extract		

- Preheat oven to 350 degrees. Grease a 10-inch tube pan.

- Blend butter, shortening and sugar until fluffy.

- Beat the eggs until they are lemon-colored; add them to the sugar mixture.

- Sift the flour and baking powder. Alternately add the dry ingredients and milk to the egg mixture. Stir in rum, butter, vanilla, coconut and lemon extracts.

- Bake for 1½ hours.

- For the glaze, combine the water, sugar and rum, butter, vanilla, coconut and lemon extracts. Boil until sugar dissolves. Pour over the hot cake. Cool the cake in the pan.

Texas Sheet Cake

Yield: approximately 40 servings

Cake

2	sticks margarine	½	teaspoon salt
1	cup water	2	eggs
4	tablespoons cocoa	½	cup sour cream
2	cups all-purpose flour	1	teaspoon baking soda
2	cups sugar		

Frosting

1	stick margarine	¾	(12-ounce) box confectioners' sugar
4	tablespoons cocoa	1	teaspoon vanilla
6	tablespoons milk		Chopped nuts (optional)

■ Preheat oven to 375 degrees. Grease an 11 x 17 x 1-inch baking sheet.

■ Bring margarine, water and cocoa to a boil and remove from heat. Stir in flour, sugar and salt. Beat in eggs, sour cream and baking soda.

■ Pour batter onto prepared baking sheet. Bake for 15 to 18 minutes on rack in the middle of the oven. Frost cake while hot.

■ For frosting, bring margarine, cocoa and milk to a boil. Remove from heat. Beat sugar and vanilla into chocolate mixture. Pour over warm cake as soon as cake is removed from oven, spreading frosting quickly.

■ Sprinkle with nuts if desired.

MISSISSIPPI MUD CAKE

Yield: 24 servings

Cake

1 cup butter
½ cup cocoa
2 cups sugar
4 eggs, beaten
1½ cups all-purpose flour

Dash salt
1½ cups chopped nuts
1 teaspoon vanilla extract
Miniature marshmallows

Chocolate Frosting

1 (16-ounce) box
    confectioners' sugar
½ cup milk

⅓ cup cocoa
¼ cup butter, softened

- Preheat oven to 350 degrees. Grease a 13 x 9-inch baking pan.

- Melt butter with cocoa. Remove from heat. Stir in sugar and eggs; mix well. Slowly add flour, salt, nuts and vanilla.

- Pour batter into prepared pan and bake for 35 to 45 minutes. Sprinkle marshmallows on top of cake.

- For frosting, combine sugar, milk, cocoa and butter. Mix until smooth.

- Spread on hot cake.

Praise be to the Lord God, the God of Israel, who alone does marvelous deeds. Praise be to his glorious name forever; may the whole earth be filled with his glory. Amen and Amen.

Psalm 72:18-19

Strawberry and White Chocolate Cake

Yield: 24 servings

1 (16-ounce) package white cake mix
1 (3-ounce) package white chocolate pudding

1 pint strawberries, washed and sliced
1 (8-ounce) container frozen nondairy whipped topping

- Prepare white cake mix according to package directions. Bake in a 9 x 13-inch baking pan. Let cool.

- Prepare white chocolate pudding according to package directions. Refrigerate.

- Sprinkle sliced strawberries with sugar to taste and refrigerate until ready to serve.

- Spread white chocolate pudding over cake. Place sliced strawberries over the pudding. Top with nondairy whipped topping.

Apricot Nectar Cake

Yield: 12 to 16 servings

Cake

1 (16-ounce) package lemon cake mix
¾ cup vegetable oil
4 eggs

½ cup granulated sugar
1 cup apricot nectar

Glaze

1½ cups confectioners' sugar, sifted
Juice of 1 lemon

½ cup apricot nectar

- Preheat oven according to cake mix directions. Spray a 10-inch fluted tube pan with cooking spray.

- Combine cake mix and oil in a large bowl. Beat in eggs one at a time. Stir in granulated sugar and nectar.

- Pour into prepared pan and bake until done in center, about 40 minutes or according to cake mix directions. Cool.

- For glaze, mix confectioners' sugar, lemon juice and nectar. Make small holes in cake with a fork. Pour glaze over cake and into holes.

Apricot nectar is available in 12-ounce cans.

Desserts—Cakes

APPLE WALNUT CAKE

Yield: 16 servings

2	cups diced apples	1¼	cups all-purpose flour
1	cup sugar	1	teaspoon ground cinnamon
1	stick unsalted butter, melted and cooled	1	teaspoon baking soda
		½	teaspoon salt
1	large egg	½	cup coarsely chopped walnuts

- Preheat oven to 375 degrees. Grease and flour an 8 x 8 x 2-inch baking pan.

- Mix apples, sugar, butter and egg in a large bowl. Sift flour, cinnamon, baking soda and salt over the apple mixture. Add the chopped walnuts and mix thoroughly.

- Pour batter into prepared pan and bake until brown and crusty on top about 45 minutes. Cake tester should come out clean after being inserted in the center of cake. Cool in the pan on a rack.

Janet Harrison has varied this recipe by using fresh peaches, blackberries or blueberries. With peaches, use almonds instead of walnuts and add 1 teaspoon almond extract. Pecans may be used also. Strawberries do not do well.

ITALIAN CREAM CAKE

Yield: 12 to 16 servings

1	(18.5-ounce) package white cake mix with pudding	3½	ounces coconut
		¼	cup vegetable oil
3	large eggs	⅔	cup chopped pecans
1¼	cups buttermilk (may substitute 1¼ cups whole milk plus 1 teaspoon lemon juice)	3	tablespoons rum, divided (optional)
		2	(16-ounce) cans vanilla frosting
		12	pecan halves

- Preheat oven to 350 degrees. Spray three 9-inch round cake pans with vegetable cooking spray.

- Beat cake mix, eggs, buttermilk and oil. Stir in coconut and pecans. Pour batter into prepared cake pans.

- Bake for 15 to 17 minutes. Cool in pans on wire racks for 10 minutes. Remove from pans and cool completely on wire racks.

- Sprinkle each layer with 1 tablespoon rum. Frost cake and garnish with pecan halves.

Desserts—Cakes   *179*

Chocolate Upside Down Cake

Yield: 16 servings

Cake

1	cup flour	½	cup milk
¾	cup sugar	2	tablespoons butter or
1½	tablespoons cocoa		margarine, melted
2	teaspoons baking powder	1	teaspoon vanilla extract
¾	teaspoon salt		

Syrup

½	cup brown sugar	1	cup hot water
½	cup white sugar	2	tablespoons cocoa

- Preheat oven to 350 degrees. Grease an 8 x 8 x 2-inch baking pan.

- Sift flour, sugar, cocoa, baking powder and salt. Stir in milk, butter and vanilla. Pour into prepared pan.

- For the sauce, boil sugars, water and cocoa about 5 minutes to make a thin syrup. Pour this over the batter and bake for 40 minutes.

- The syrup sinks to the bottom and thickens as the cake bakes. Serve warm, upside-down with whipped cream or ice cream.

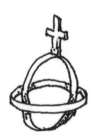

*B*LUEBERRY *T*EA *C*AKE

Yield: 16 servings

Cake

¼ cup softened butter
¾ cup sugar
1 egg, beaten
½ cup milk

2 cups all-purpose flour
2 teaspoons baking powder
½ teaspoon salt
2 cups blueberries

Topping

½ cup sugar
¼ cup flour

½ teaspoon cinnamon
¼ cup softened butter

- Preheat oven to 375 degrees. Grease an 8 x 8-inch baking pan.

- Blend the butter and gradually beat in the sugar. Add the egg and milk and beat until smooth.

- Sift the flour, baking powder and salt. Add to the sugar mixture. Fold in the blueberries. Spread the batter in the prepared pan.

- For crumb topping, mix sugar, flour, cinnamon and butter. Sprinkle over the batter. Bake for 40 to 45 minutes.

*C*OCONUT *C*AKE

Yield: 16-18 servings

1 (16-ounce) box yellow cake mix
16 ounces sour cream
¾ cup sugar

12 ounces frozen coconut
8 ounces frozen nondairy whipped topping, thawed

- Bake cake mix according to package directions in two 8-inch round cake pans. Cool and carefully slice each layer in half, laterally, making 4 layers.

- Mix the sour cream, sugar and coconut. Set aside 1 cup of this mixture and refrigerate. Spread the remaining mixture between the cake layers.

- Add nondairy whipped topping to the refrigerated sour cream mixture. Ice top and sides of cake. Refrigerate in an airtight container for 3 days.

BASIC *1-2-3-4* CAKE WITH CARAMEL WALNUT ICING

Yield: 16 to 20 servings

Cake

1	cup butter, softened	3	teaspoons baking powder
2	cups sugar	½	teaspoon salt
3	cups all-purpose flour, sifted	1	cup milk
4	eggs	1	teaspoon vanilla extract

Caramel Walnut Icing

2	sticks butter	3-4	cups confectioners' sugar, sifted well
2	cups firmly packed light brown sugar		
1	cup evaporated milk	1	cup finely chopped black walnuts
1	teaspoon vanilla extract		

■ Preheat oven to 350 degrees. Grease and flour three 9-inch cake pans.

■ Blend the butter with the sugar, adding the sugar gradually. Beat until light and fluffy.

■ In another bowl, sift flour, baking powder and salt.

■ Add eggs to butter and sugar one at a time, beating after each addition.

■ Add flour mixture alternately with milk to sugar and egg mixture, beating after each addition until smooth. Add vanilla.

■ Pour cake batter into three prepared cake pans and bake for 25 to 30 minutes.

■ For icing, melt butter in 3-quart saucepan. Add brown sugar and evaporated milk. Stir constantly over medium heat for 5 minutes until mixture is smooth and hot.

■ Remove from heat and add vanilla. Gradually add confectioners' sugar until spreading consistency is reached, beating well. Stir in walnuts.

$\mathcal{B}$LUE $\mathcal{R}$IBBON $\mathcal{S}$URPRISE $\mathcal{C}$AKE

Yield: 16 to 20 servings

Cake

3	cups all-purpose flour	1	cup chopped nuts
2	cups sugar	1¼	cups cooking oil
1	teaspoon salt	3	eggs
1	teaspoon baking soda	½	teaspoon vanilla extract
2½	cups diced bananas	½	teaspoon coconut extract
1	(8-ounce) can crushed pineapple		

Frosting

8	ounces cream cheese	1	cup chopped pecans
1	stick butter or margarine	2	teaspoons vanilla extract
1	box confectioners' sugar		

- Preheat oven to 325 degrees. Grease and flour three 8 or 9-inch round cake pans.

- Sift the flour, sugar, salt and baking soda.

- Make a hole in the middle of the sifted ingredients. Add bananas, undrained crushed pineapple, nuts, cooking oil, eggs, vanilla and coconut extracts. Blend well with a wooden spoon but do not beat.

- Pour batter into prepared pans. Bake for 25 minutes or until done.

- For frosting, combine cream cheese, butter, confectioners' sugar, pecans and vanilla. Beat well.

- Spread between layers and on the top and sides of the cake.

$\mathcal{L}$EMON $\mathcal{I}$CEBOX $\mathcal{C}$AKE

Yield: 12 to 16 servings

Cake

6	eggs, separated	1	(3¼-ounce) envelope unflavored gelatin
¾	cup sugar		
¾	cup lemon juice	¾	cup white corn syrup
1½	teaspoons lemon zest	1	angel food cake, broken into pieces

Frosting

2   cups heavy cream   Sugar to taste
Vanilla extract to taste

- ▪ Grease a 9 or 10-inch tube pan.

- ▪ Mix egg yolks, sugar, lemon juice and zest in a double boiler until mixture reaches consistency of custard.

- ▪ Soften unflavored gelatin in ¼ cup cold water and add to custard. Beat egg whites until stiff. Add corn syrup to egg whites, beating constantly. Add to custard.

- ▪ Layer custard and angel food cake in tube pan, beginning and ending with custard. Refrigerate overnight.

- ▪ The next day, whip the cream. Add vanilla and sugar to taste. Ice the cake.

OLIVE FRUIT

Hummingbird Cake

Yield: 12 to 16 servings

Cake

3 cups all-purpose flour	3 eggs, well beaten
1 teaspoon salt	1 (8-ounce) can crushed pineapple
1 teaspoon baking soda	1 cup chopped walnuts or pecans
1 teaspoon cinnamon	4 bananas, chopped
2 cups sugar	1½ teaspoons vanilla extract
1½ cups vegetable oil	

Frosting

2 (8-ounce) packages cream cheese, softened	2 (16-ounce) boxes confectioners' sugar
½ pound butter or margarine, softened	2 teaspoons vanilla extract
	1 cup chopped walnuts or pecans

■ Preheat oven to 350 degrees. Grease and flour three 8 or 9-inch cake pans.

■ Sift flour, salt, baking soda and cinnamon. Stir in sugar, then oil and eggs until all dry ingredients are moistened.

■ Fold in pineapple, nuts, bananas and vanilla but do not beat.

■ Spoon batter into prepared cake pans. Bake for 25 to 30 minutes.

■ Cool cake in cake pans for 10 minutes. Remove from pans and cool completely.

■ For frosting, blend the cream cheese and butter. Beat in confectioners' sugar until icing is light and fluffy. Stir in vanilla and mix again.

■ Frost the cake layers and sprinkle with nuts.

LIGHTENED HUMMINGBIRD CAKE

Yield: 20 servings

Cake

Vegetable cooking spray
3 cups plus 2 teaspoons all-purpose flour, divided
1 teaspoon baking soda
½ teaspoon salt
1¾ cups sugar
1 teaspoon cinnamon

2 large eggs
½ cup unsweetened applesauce
3 tablespoons vegetable oil
1¾ cups mashed banana (about 5-6)
1½ teaspoons vanilla extract
1 (8-ounce) can crushed pineapple, undrained

Frosting

1 (8-ounce) package reduced-fat cream cheese, unsoftened
1 (3-ounce) package cream cheese, softened

1 tablespoon light butter, unsoftened
6 cups powdered sugar
1 teaspoon vanilla extract
¾ cup chopped pecans

■ Preheat oven to 350 degrees. Coat three 9-inch round cake pans with cooking spray. Sprinkle 2 teaspoons flour evenly into pans, shaking to coat.

■ Combine remaining 3 cups flour and baking soda, salt, sugar and cinnamon. Blend eggs, applesauce and oil. Add to flour mixture, stirring until dry ingredients are moistened. (Do not beat.) Stir in mashed banana, vanilla and pineapple. Pour batter evenly into prepared pans.

■ Bake for 23 to 25 minutes or until a wooden pick inserted in center comes out clean.

■ Cool layers in pans on wire racks for 10 minutes. Remove layers from pans and cool completely on wire racks.

■ For frosting, beat cream cheese and butter at high speed with an electric mixer until creamy.

■ Gradually add powdered sugar and beat at low speed until smooth.

■ Stir in vanilla and pecans.

Desserts—Cakes

OLETA'S TORTE

Yield: 8 to 12 servings

Cake
1	(16¼-ounce) package brownie mix	¼	cup water
		¼	cup cooking oil
3	eggs	½	cup chopped nuts

Frosting
2	cups heavy cream	½	cup firmly packed brown sugar
1	tablespoon instant coffee		
Small amount water		Pecan halves	

- Preheat oven to 350 degrees. Grease two 9-inch round cake pans.

- Prepare brownie mix by combining mix, eggs, water, oil and nuts according to package directions. Pour into prepared cake pans and bake for 20 minutes until a toothpick inserted in the middle comes out clean. Cool.

- For frosting, whip the cream until it begins to thicken. Mix instant coffee with a small amount of water to form a paste. Gradually add coffee paste and brown sugar to whipped cream. Continue whipping cream until it reaches spreading consistency.

- Spread between the layers and on sides and top of brownie cake. Garnish with pecan halves. Chill overnight.

Be devoted to one another in brotherly love. Honor one another above yourselves. Never be lacking in zeal, but keep your spiritual fervor, serving the Lord. Be joyful in hope, patient in affliction, faithful in prayer. Share with God's people who are in need. Practice hospitality.

Romans 12:10-13

Big Jim's Chocolate Cake

Yield: 8 to 12 servings

Big Jim was James H. Gordon, Sr. He was a life long member of Galilee and served on the vestry. He used to make this cake on Sunday when the Spirit moved him. It was an old-fashioned, heavy, moist cake.

Cake

2	sticks butter	1	cup milk
2	cups sugar	1	teaspoon vanilla extract
4	eggs, separated	3	teaspoons baking powder
3	cups sifted all-purpose flour		

Chocolate Icing

½	stick butter	1	egg, beaten
2	cups sugar	Milk	
3	squares unsweetened chocolate		

- Preheat oven to 350 degrees. Grease and flour two 9-inch cake pans.

- Blend butter and sugar. Beat in egg yolks. Alternately stir in flour and milk. Add vanilla and baking powder. Beat batter by hand for 2 minutes. Fold in 4 stiffly beaten egg whites. Pour batter into prepared pans.

- Bake 30 minutes.

- For icing, cook butter, sugar, chocolate and egg on low heat and stir occasionally. If necessary add milk for moisture. The icing is done when soft ball forms in a cup of cold water.

- Cool slightly and then beat until shiny (this is very important). Scoop the soft icing onto cake and spread while still warm.

SOUTHERN COMFORT CAKE

Yield: Approximately 16 servings

1	box white or yellow cake mix	1	cup milk
1	package instant vanilla pudding	½	cup vegetable oil
4	ounces Southern Comfort	1	cup chopped nuts (optional)
4	eggs		

Glaze

6	tablespoons butter	¼	cup sugar
¾	cup Southern Comfort		

- ■ Preheat oven to 325 degrees. Grease and flour a 10-inch tube pan.

- ■ Beat cake mix, pudding, Southern Comfort and eggs. Add milk and oil.

- ■ Pour batter into tube pan and bake for 60 minutes. Leave cake in pan.

- ■ For glaze, combine butter, Southern Comfort and sugar in a saucepan. Cook over medium heat until bubbling and butter is melted.

- ■ Make holes in the top of the cake with a cake tester or toothpick. Pour glaze over hot cake in pan.

- ■ Cool for 2 hours. Remove cake from pan and wrap in foil. Refrigerate for at least 24 hours, the longer the better.

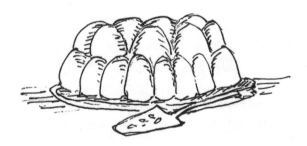

Desserts—Cakes

Nana Bruce's Ginger Snaps

Yield: 4 dozen

1	cup molasses	2	teaspoons baking soda
1	cup sugar	1	teaspoon ginger
1	cup butter	2	teaspoons cinnamon
¼	cup hot water	4	cups all-purpose flour

- Combine molasses, sugar, butter, water, baking soda, ginger, cinnamon and flour.
- Form a roll and wrap in waxed paper. Refrigerate overnight.
- To bake, preheat oven to 350 degrees.
- Slice dough very thin. Place rounds on baking sheet. Bake for 10 minutes.

Lemon Cookies

Yield: 1½ dozen

½	pound butter	1	teaspoon lemon extract
1	cup sugar	1⅛-1¼	cups all-purpose flour
2	egg yolks	1	teaspoon salt
Grated rind of 1 lemon			

- Blend butter and sugar. Add egg yolks, grated lemon rind and lemon extract. Sift flour and salt into the mixture. Mix and chill the dough.
- Preheat oven to 350 degrees.
- Drop by teaspoon onto baking sheet. Press each cookie with a fork dipped in sugar to make 3 ridges. Leave plenty of room between cookies as they will spread.
- Bake until cookies begin to brown around the edges, 5 to 10 minutes.

Oatmeal Cookies

Yield: 1½ dozen

1	stick butter or margarine	1	egg, beaten
1	cup light brown sugar	1	cup quick-cooking oats
1	teaspoon vanilla	½	cup all-purpose flour
Dash salt			

- Preheat oven to 350 degrees. Grease a baking sheet.

- Blend butter and brown sugar. Beat in vanilla, salt, egg, oats and flour. Drop by half-teaspoon on prepared baking sheet.

- Bake for 6 minutes.

Sugar Cookies

Yield: 9 to 10 dozen

1	cup sugar	1	teaspoon baking soda
2	sticks butter, softened	1	teaspoon cream of tartar
2	eggs	¼	teaspoon salt
1	teaspoon vanilla	1	cup oil
5	cups all-purpose flour	1	cup confectioners' sugar

- Preheat oven to 375 degrees.

- Mix sugar, butter, eggs and vanilla at low speed. Combine flour, baking soda, cream of tartar and salt. Alternating the dry ingredients with the oil, gradually beat into sugar mixture.

- Roll dough into balls the size of a nickel. Place on ungreased baking sheet. Flatten each with the bottom of a small glass dipped in sugar.

- Bake for 10 to 15 minutes.

Sugar cookies freeze well.

Skillet Cookies

Yield: 3 to 4 dozen

1	stick butter or margarine	2	cups crisp rice cereal
2	eggs	½	cup chopped nuts
1	cup sugar	1	teaspoon vanilla extract
1	(8-ounce) package dates, chopped	1	cup shredded or flaked coconut

- Melt butter or margarine in a saucepan. Beat eggs and sugar and add to melted butter. Fold in dates.

- Bring mixture to a boil, then reduce heat to low. Stirring constantly, cook about 6 minutes.

- Remove from heat. Stir in crisp rice cereal, nuts and vanilla. Allow mixture to cool.

- Drop by heaping teaspoons into coconut. Roll into balls.

FLAX

Chocolate Butterscotch Drop Cookies

Yield: 3 dozen

12	ounces semisweet chocolate	1½	cups salted peanuts
12	ounces butterscotch morsels	1	(5-ounce) can Chinese noodles

- Melt the chocolate and butterscotch morsels in the top of a double boiler. Add the peanuts and noodles and stir well.

- Drop the mixture by rounded teaspoons onto waxed paper. Allow to stand until hard.

Desserts—Cookies and Bars

FLOSSIE'S FUDGE COOKIES

Yield: 2 dozen

1   (12-ounce) package chocolate
    morsels
2   tablespoons butter
1   (14-ounce) can sweetened
    condensed milk

1   cup all-purpose flour
½   cup chopped nuts

■ Preheat oven to 325 degrees. Lightly grease baking sheets.

■ Melt chocolate morsels and butter in top of double boiler. Blend in condensed milk. Stir in flour and nuts, mixing well. Keep mixture warm.

■ Drop by teaspoon on prepared baking sheets. Bake 5 minutes. Cool.

WHITE CHOCOLATE ORANGE CREAM COOKIES

Yield: 3½ dozen

1   cup softened butter
¾   cup light brown sugar
½   cup granulated sugar
1   egg
1   tablespoon grated orange rind

2   teaspoons orange extract
2¼ cups all-purpose flour
¾   teaspoon baking soda
½   teaspoon salt
2   cups white chocolate morsels

■ Preheat oven to 350 degrees.

■ Beat butter, brown sugar and granulated sugar until creamy. Add egg, orange rind and orange extract. Beat until smooth.

■ Combine the flour, baking soda and salt. Gradually beat into the butter mixture. Stir in the chocolate morsels.

■ Drop onto ungreased baking sheet. Bake for 10 to 12 minutes. Cool for 2 minutes then remove to rack.

$\mathcal{A}$LMOND $\mathcal{S}$QUARES

Yield: 2 dozen

Squares

¼ cup butter
¼ cup shortening

1 cup all-purpose flour
2 tablespoons confectioners' sugar

Topping

1¼ cups brown sugar
2 tablespoons all-purpose flour
2 eggs, beaten

¾ cup chopped almonds
¾ cup grated coconut
1 teaspoon almond extract

- Preheat oven to 400 degrees. Grease an 11 x 7 x 2-inch pan.

- Cream butter and shortening until well blended. Mix in flour and confectioners' sugar until crumbly. Press into baking pan and bake for 10 minutes.

- For topping, combine the brown sugar, flour, eggs, almonds, coconut and almond extracts. Spread over the baked dough and continue baking for 20 minutes. When cool, sprinkle with confectioners' sugar and cut into squares.

$\mathcal{Y}$UMMY $\mathcal{L}$EMON $\mathcal{B}$ARS

Yield: 16 bars

1 cup plus 2 tablespoons
  all-purpose flour,
  divided
½ cup butter
½ cup confectioners' sugar,
  divided

1 cup sugar
2 eggs, beaten
½ teaspoon baking powder
3 tablespoons lemon juice
Grated rind of 1 lemon

- Preheat oven to 350 degrees.

- Mix 1 cup flour, butter and ¼ cup confectioners' sugar. Press this mixture into an 8 x 8 x 2-inch pan and bake 18 minutes.

- Mix sugar, eggs, 2 tablespoons flour, baking powder, lemon juice and lemon rind. Pour over the crust and bake for 25 minutes.

- Sprinkle with remaining confectioners' sugar while warm.

$\mathcal{A}$RKANSAS $\mathcal{B}$ROWNIES

Yield: 1½ to 2 dozen

2	sticks butter or margarine	1	cup all-purpose flour
4	squares unsweetened chocolate	¼	teaspoon salt
4	eggs	1	teaspoon vanilla
2	cups sugar	2	cups chopped pecans or walnuts

◾ Preheat oven to 350 degrees. Melt butter and chocolate in a 9 x 13 x 2-inch baking pan.

◾ Beat the eggs in a mixing bowl and add the sugar, melted butter and chocolate, flour, salt and vanilla. Fold in the nuts and return the mixture to the baking pan. Bake for 30 to 45 minutes. Do not over bake. Cut while warm.

$\mathcal{A}$LMOND $\mathcal{R}$OCA $\mathcal{S}$QUARES

Yield: 3 to 4 dozen

1	cup butter	1	teaspoon vanilla extract
¾	cup brown sugar	2	cups all-purpose flour
½	cup granulated sugar	16	ounces semisweet chocolate
1	egg yolk, beaten		Blanched almond slivers

◾ Preheat oven to 350 degrees. Grease a 15 x 10-inch baking sheet.

◾ Blend butter, brown sugar, white sugar, egg yolk, vanilla and flour.

◾ Spread dough over prepared baking sheet. Bake 15 to 20 minutes.

◾ Melt chocolate in a double boiler. Spread over hot crust. Sprinkle with almonds. Cut into squares while hot.

CHOCOLATE CARAMEL BROWNIES

Yield: 2 dozen

1 (16-ounce) German chocolate cake mix	⅔ cup evaporated milk, divided
¾ cup butter, melted	1 (14-ounce) package caramel candies
	6 ounces chocolate morsels

■ Preheat oven to 350 degrees. Grease a 9 x 13 x 2-inch baking pan.

■ Combine the cake mix, butter and ⅓ cup milk. Spread ½ the mixture into the prepared pan and bake for 6 minutes.

■ Melt the caramels in the remaining milk. Sprinkle the chocolate morsels over the first layer of baked brownies. Drizzle the caramels and milk over the morsels.

■ Spread remaining cake mixture over top. Bake for 15 to 18 minutes. Cool brownies before cutting.

OUTRAGEOUS CHOCOLATE BARS

Yield: 36 bars or 2 dozen cookies

½ cup granulated sugar	1 cup all-purpose flour
⅓ cup packed brown sugar	½ cup rolled oats
½ cup butter or margarine, softened	1 teaspoon baking soda
½ teaspoon vanilla extract	¼ teaspoon salt
½ cup peanut butter	1 (6-ounce) package semisweet chocolate morsels
1 egg	

■ Preheat oven to 350 degrees. Grease a 9 x 9 x 2-inch baking dish for bars or use ungreased baking sheets for drop cookies.

■ Beat the granulated sugar, brown sugar, butter, vanilla, peanut butter and egg in a medium-sized mixing bowl until creamy and well-blended. Stir in flour, oats, baking soda and salt. Fold in chocolate morsels.

■ For bars, spread dough evenly in prepared baking dish. Bake 25 to 30 minutes. When cool, cut into 2 x 1-inch bars.

■ For cookies, drop dough from a teaspoon onto the ungreased baking sheet. Bake for 10 to 12 minutes. Cool for 1 minute before removing from pan.

KILLER BOURBON BALLS

Yield: 4 dozen

3	cups finely crushed vanilla wafers	2	cups finely chopped pecans, divided
2	cups confectioners' sugar, divided	3	tablespoons corn syrup
1	tablespoon cocoa	6	ounces bourbon

■ Combine wafer crumbs, 1 cup sugar, cocoa, 1 cup pecans, corn syrup and bourbon. Mix until thoroughly blended.

■ Roll dough into small balls. Combine remaining sugar and pecans and spread on a plate. Roll the balls in the mixture to coat. Chill thoroughly and store in an airtight container.

The original recipe called for 6 tablespoons of bourbon. Kitty Williams mistakenly made them with 6 ounces of bourbon and got rave reviews; she continues to use 6 ounces.

SWEDISH BUTTERBALLS

Yield: 4½ dozen

½	pound butter	1	cup finely chopped pecans
¾-1	cup confectioners' sugar, divided	2	cups all-purpose flour
1	teaspoon vanilla extract		

■ Preheat oven to 325 degrees.

■ Blend butter and ½ cup sugar. Stir in vanilla, pecans and flour. Form into walnut-sized balls. Roll in remaining sugar.

■ Bake 20 to 30 minutes.

MOTHER'S MERINGUE KISSES

Yield: 6 dozen

3 egg whites	1 teaspoon lemon juice
1 cup sugar	¾ cup toasted slivered almonds

- Preheat oven to 250 degrees. Grease baking sheets.

- Beat egg whites until stiff. Add sugar slowly and beat until very stiff. Fold in lemon juice and toasted almonds.

- Drop by rounded teaspoons onto baking sheets. Bake for 45 minutes.

ORANGE BLOSSOMS

Yield: 5 dozen

Cupcakes

½ cup butter	2 cups all-purpose flour
1½ cups sugar	1½ teaspoons baking powder
½ teaspoon vanilla extract	3 eggs
½ teaspoon lemon extract	¾ cup milk
½ teaspoon almond extract	

Glaze

1¼ pounds confectioners' sugar	Juice of 2 oranges
Juice of 2 lemons	Grated rind of 2 oranges
Grated rind of 1 lemon	

- Preheat oven to 425 degrees. Grease small muffin tins.

- Cream butter and sugar. Add eggs, vanilla, lemon and almond extracts. Sift flour and baking powder. Gradually add to the sugar mixture, alternating with milk. Mix thoroughly. Spoon into prepared tins, 1 teaspoon per cup.

- Bake for 8 minutes.

- For glaze, combine confectioners' sugar, lemon juice, lemon rind, orange juice and orange rind. Mix well.

- Dip hot cupcakes into the glaze.

$\mathcal{B}$LUEBERRY $\mathcal{T}$ORTE

Yield: 8 servings

½ cup butter	2 eggs
1 cup sugar	1 pint blueberries
1 cup all-purpose flour	¼ cup sugar
1 teaspoon baking powder	Juice of 1 lemon
Pinch of salt	Cinnamon to cover

- Preheat oven to 350 degrees. Blend the butter and sugar. Sift flour, baking powder and salt and add to the butter and sugar mixture. Beat in 2 eggs.

- Place the mixture in a 9-inch springform pan. Cover with the blueberries. Sprinkle the berries with sugar, lemon juice and cinnamon. Bake for 1 hour.

Best served warm with whipped cream or ice cream.

$\mathcal{B}$OILED $\mathcal{C}$USTARD

Yield: 4 servings

3 egg yolks	2 cups whole milk, heated
¼ cup sugar	½ teaspoon vanilla
Pinch salt	

- Beat egg yolks slightly. Add the sugar and salt to beaten yolks. Gradually stir in hot milk. Cook in the top of a double boiler, stirring constantly until the custard thickens and coats the spoon.

- Cool the custard and add the vanilla. If the custard separates, put it in a pan of cold water at once and beat it until smooth.

BOB BEASLEY'S PEACH ICE CREAM

Yield: 8 servings

1   quart peeled and mashed   3   cups sugar
    peaches   1   teaspoon vanilla
1   quart half-and-half

■ Combine the mashed peaches, half-and-half, sugar and vanilla. Chill.

■ Pour ice cream custard into ice cream freezer. Follow the freezer's directions.

Come Lord Jesus,
Be our guest,
And let these gifts to us be blessed;
And may there be a goodly share
On every table, everywhere.
Amen

One of the four prayers said by Barbara Principe's daughters.

LEMON CHIFFON

Yield: 6 to 8 servings

Juice of 3 lemons   1   cup sugar (very fine)
Grated rind of 3 lemons   1   pint whipping cream

■ Mix the lemon juice and grated rind with the sugar until the sugar is dissolved.

■ Whip the cream and add to the lemon mixture. Freeze.

Desserts—Miscellaneous

MRS. NASH'S PRUNE WHIP

Yield: 4 to 6 servings

1	cup pitted prunes, cooked and chopped	1	teaspoon all-purpose flour
1	cup sugar	6	egg whites
			Pinch salt

- Preheat oven to 350 degrees.

- Combine the prunes, sugar and flour in a small bowl.

- In a large bowl, beat the egg whites until stiff but not dry. Blend in prunes by hand. Pour into a 3-quart casserole with straight sides and place in a pan of hot water approximately 1 inch deep. Bake 40 to 60 minutes. Serve hot with custard.

Prepared strained prunes for babies can be used.

DIRT PUDDING

Yield: 8 to 10 servings

2	cups cold milk	8-10 (7-ounce) clear plastic cups or a large glass bowl
1	(4-ounce) box instant chocolate pudding	Gummy worms, gummy spiders, candy flowers (optional)
8	ounces frozen whipped topping, thawed	
1	(16-ounce) package chocolate sandwich cookies, crushed and divided	

- Pour milk into a large bowl and add the chocolate pudding mix. Beat with a whisk or hand mixer until well blended. Let stand for 5 minutes. Stir in thawed whipped topping and ½ the crushed cookies.

- Place 1 tablespoon of the crushed cookies into the bottom of each cup or make a layer of crushed cookies in the bottom of a glass bowl. Fill the cups or bowl ¾ full with the pudding mixture. Top with the remaining cookies.

- Refrigerate for 1 hour and add the gummy worms, spiders or flowers, if desired.

Jo Elliott's Cream Grapes

Yield: 4 servings

4 cups seedless green grapes	½ cup brown sugar
1 cup sour cream	

- Combine sour cream and brown sugar. Pour over grapes and thoroughly mix.
- Marinate grapes in sour cream mixture for at least 2 hours. Serve cold with a light, thin cookie.

Wine Jelly Dessert

Yield: 16 servings

2 tablespoons granulated gelatin	⅓ cup orange juice
½ cup water	3 tablespoons lemon juice
1½ cups boiling water	Whipped topping and cherries for
1 cup sugar	garnish
1 cup dry sherry	

- Dissolve gelatin in ½ cup water. Add the boiling water, sugar, sherry, orange juice and lemon juice to the gelatin.
- Refrigerate until gelatin is firmly set. Top with whipped topping and a cherry.

$\mathcal{L}$U'S $\mathcal{L}$EMON $\mathcal{I}$CE $\mathcal{C}$REAM $\mathcal{T}$ORTE

Yield: 10 servings

½ cup butter or margarine
2 teaspoons grated lemon rind
⅓ cup lemon juice
¼ teaspoon salt
1 cup sugar

3 eggs, beaten
1 thinly sliced frozen pound cake
½ gallon vanilla ice cream, softened
    slightly

- Melt the butter and add the lemon zest, lemon juice, salt and sugar. Fold in the beaten eggs.

- Cook until thick and smooth, stirring frequently. Cool lemon mixture completely.

- Layer slices of frozen cake, ice cream, and sauce in a 2-quart casserole dish or glass dish or bowl. Finish the layering by swirling sauce over the top.

$\mathcal{Q}$UEEN OF $\mathcal{P}$UDDINGS

Yield: 6 servings

3⅓ cups stale bread, crusts removed
     and cubed
3 cups milk, heated
3 egg yolks, beaten
¾ cup sugar plus 6 tablespoons sugar,
    divided

Juice of 1 lemon, divided
Grated rind of 1 lemon, divided
Damson plum preserves
3 egg whites
⅛ teaspoon salt

- Preheat oven to 350 degrees. Grease a 2-quart round baking dish.

- Soak bread cubes in heated milk for 15 minutes. Stir in egg yolks, ¾ cup sugar, half the lemon juice, and half the lemon rind.

- Place baking dish in a pan of hot water and bake for 30 to 45 minutes, being careful not to overcook.

- Spread preserves over the top of the pudding.

- Beat egg whites until fluffy. Stir in 6 tablespoons sugar, salt, remaining lemon juice and remaining lemon rind. Spread over the preserves. Return to oven and bake until slightly brown.

Ice Cream Custard

Yield: 24 servings

2 quarts whole milk	8 eggs, beaten
2 cups sugar	1 (5-ounce) can evaporated milk

- Combine the whole milk, sugar, eggs and evaporated milk and cook until thickened, or until mixture reaches 180 degrees on a candy thermometer. Be careful not to boil.
- Put into a 6-quart freezer. Freeze.

To make peach custard add 12 mashed peaches, sugar to taste and ¼ teaspoon almond extract.

Grand Marnier Soufflé

Yield: 6 to 8 servings

Vanilla wafers to cover bottom of soufflé dish	⅓ cup all-purpose flour
½ cup milk	½ cup sugar
6 tablespoons Grand Marnier liqueur, divided	1½ cups half-and-half cream
½ cup milk	3 egg yolks, slightly beaten
1 teaspoon vanilla extract	6 egg whites, stiffly beaten
¼ cup butter	8 ounces heavy cream, whipped

- Preheat oven to 425 degrees. Grease a 2 to 3-quart soufflé dish.
- Arrange vanilla wafers on the bottom of the soufflé dish. Pour 4 tablespoons liqueur over them.
- Microwave the milk for 1 minute. Add the vanilla to milk.
- Melt butter in the top of a double boiler. Stir in the flour to make a smooth paste. Add the milk and sugar alternately, stirring constantly to make a smooth paste. Pour in the cream, stirring constantly until smooth and creamy.
- Remove from heat. Slowly stir egg yolks into about ¼ of the hot mixture. Mix 1 tablespoon liqueur into the mixture thoroughly.
- Cool mixture. Fold in ¼ of the egg whites using a wire whisk. Thoroughly fold in remaining egg whites. Pour mixture over vanilla wafers.
- Bake for 25 to 30 minutes or until soufflé has puffed, set and browned.
- Stir 1 tablespoon liqueur into the whipped cream. Serve immediately with a spoon of whipped cream on top.

Desserts—Miscellaneous

$\mathcal{P}$ATRONS

Mrs. Polly Altizer

St. John Arnold

Mr. and Mrs. Keith Barber

Mr. and Mrs. Thomas Barnes

Ann Beasley

Polly Bechard

Jeannette P. Blake

Mr. and Mrs. David Brockwell

Helen Brothers

Betty Jo Bruce

Laura T. Cook

Mr. and Mrs. Sheldon Corner

Mr. and Mrs. Al Davis

Mr. and Mrs. Winston Davis

Mr. and Mrs. Shepherd Drewry, Jr.

Donna A. Eure

Jane LeCompte Evans

Mrs. Genevieve Galliford

Mr. and Mrs. Michael Gomez

Juliet L. Goode

Mr. and Mrs. Lewis B. Goode, Jr.

William Goodwin, Jr.

Mr. and Mrs. Patrick Gravitt

Mary Donnan Harrison

Mr. and Mrs. W. R. Hemingway

Rose Hess

Terri Hewitt

Mr. and Mrs. T. J. Howard, Jr.

Pamela Hutchins

Jerrie H. Hyle

Mr. and Mrs. William John

Cheryl Jordan

Rev. and Mrs. John Jordon

Mr. and Mrs. James Kitchin, Jr.

Betty Herbert Koch

Mr. and Mrs. Rudolph H. Koch

Mr. and Mrs. Thomas Lyons

Mr. and Mrs. Scott Mason

John McClain

Margaret Mordecai

Elizabeth Munford

Anne Overman

Edythe Owen

Douglass Patterson

Carolyn Payne

Mr. and Mrs. Dan Proulx

Jane M. Purrington

Ann Randolph

Laura Rawls

John Richardson

Kay Richardson

Lisa D. Robertson

Hardy Robinson

Winifred Russell

Dr. Susan F. Sandler

Jane Sautter

Margery Standing

Mr. and Mrs. Franklin Tuck

Mary Tyler

Mr. and Mrs. Roger Visser

Katherine Williams

We regret the omission of those who
submitted donations after September 20, 2004.

Contributors

Tricia Ailstock
Barbara Airing
Aldo's
Polly Altizer
Diane Ames
Alma Anderson
Bobbie Aucamp (deceased)
Shelby Balderson
Betty Barco
Claudy Barnes
Bob Beasley (deceased)
Bella Monte
Belvedere
Joan Berlin
Jodi Berndt
Alice Bishop
Marian L. C. Blair
Lugean Boice
Ami Bondi
Betty Bradshaw
Debbie Brady
Ann Bragg
Helen Brothers
Betty Jo Bruce
Norvell Butler
Rhonda Byrd
Ann Callis
Charlotte Carter
Kerri Jean Carter
Cavalier Yacht and Country Club
Christiana Campbell's Tavern
Alba I. M. Clare
Kathleen Coalter
Betty Lew Coleman
Theresa Cook
Dana Darden Copeland
June Corner (deceased)
Shel Corner
Martha Cotten
Sharon Cowan
Coyote Café
Kitty Crittenden

Cypress Point Country Club
Mary Lou Darden
Jewel Davis
Rosalie Delaney
Jane Denman
Mary Dickinson
Anne Donahoe
Pat DuBois
Pat Dunthorn
Elizabeth Dye
Shelly Farley
Betty Fitts
Karen Fletcher
Bonnie Folck
Mary Folck
Marie Folck
Jean A. Ford
Teedie Ganzel
Anne Gentry
Irvin Gentry
Beverly Gilliam
Margaret Gilliam
Carl Gilmer
Phyllis Gimbert
Marietta Glascock
Rosemary Gomez
Suzanne Gravitt
Tris Graybeal
Phyliss Grubbs
Claudia Gunter
Janet P. Harrison
Helen Henderson
Betty D. Hodges
Pat Holland
Carol Holmes
Evie Holt
Myrnie Howard
Il Giardino
Anne Jarrett
Lucy Jones
Missy Jones
Anne Jordan
Cheryl Jordan

CONTRIBUTORS

Dickie Jordan
Robbin Jordan
Betsy Keen
Betty Kernan
Vicki Kigerl
Donna Killen
Nancy Kimball
Susan Kirchner
Jennie Kitchin
Mrs. W. H. Kitchin
Joan Lee
Doris Lindeman (deceased)
Linda Lindfors
Lynne Lindsay
Jacqueline Lucas
Lucky Star, Chef Amy Brandt
Mahi Mah's
Dixie Mallison (deceased)
Pat Mann
Betty Driver McCaa
Gwen Meredith
Betty Miles
Alice Miles
Mariah's at Tower Hill
Mary Lou Morris
Betsy Munford
A. E. "Jack" Murray
Sis Nash (deceased)
Fontaine Nimmo
Allison Neumann
Betsy Nugent
Anne W. O'Connor
Anne Overman
Louise Pearson
Cathryn Perry
Gina Pitrone
C. Sherry Potts
Jeanne Preston
Wendy Preston
Princess Anne Country Club
Barbara Principe
Pat Proulx

Purple Cow
Jean Marie Randolph
Laura Rawls
Flossie Reinhardt
Kay Richardson
Hardy Robinson
Ross Robinson
Kit Roller
Jodi Rose
Alice Rueger
Mollie Rueger
Claire Rundle
Jane Sautter
Kay Scarborough
Cecil Schwartz
Emily Slingluff
Rita Angell Spitzli
Steinhilber's Thalia Acres Inn
Bettye Sterzing
Ann Taylor
Mrs. R. B. Taylor
Carol Temple
Tournament Players Club of Virginia
    Beach, Chef Chris Ghalaxini
Jo Trant
Travis House
Ann Troiano
Mary Sallé Tyler
Stockton H. Tyler (deceased)
Cass Veasey
Elizabeth Ward
Elizabeth Ware
Mary Waters
Richard Welton (deceased)
Marti Whelan
Marcia Wheeler
Lu Wiley
Kitty Williams
Williamsburg Inn
Dale Wilson
Nancy Wolcott
Ann Wright
Margaret Zontini

LOAVES AND FISHES COMMITTEE MEMBERS

Polly Altizer

Alma Anderson

Sarah Atherholt

Claudy Barnes

Ginny Bell

Libby Bennett

Betsy Brown

Carole Brown

Rhonda Byrd

Bill Campbell

Jewel Davis

Jane Denman

Mary Dickinson

Jane LeCompte Evans

Mary Folck

Suzanne Ganschinietz
  (Editor and Co-Chair)

Margaret Gilliam

Lori Goldwag

Diane Hayes

Phyllis Hayes

Pat Holland

Molly Ill

Missy Jones

Liz Keane

Betsy Keen

Donna Killen

Marian Kitchin (Editor)

Karen Lindvall

Jacquelyn Lucas

Pat Mann

Don Monteaux

Betty Driver McCaa

Sara Moore

Mary Lou Morris

Fontaine Nimmo

Anne Overman

Douglass Patterson

Jeanne Preston

Pat Proulx

Hardy Robinson

Kit Roller

Gay Lynn Roundtree

Jane Sautter

Fleecie Smith

Lorna St. George (Editor)

Molly Warren

Bonnie Wheeler

Kitty Williams

Dale Wilson (Co-chair)

Index   *211*

Index   213

Index

Index   *217*

S

Index 219

MAIL TO: LOAVES & FISHES, Vol. 5
GALILEE GIFTS, 3928 PACIFIC AVENUE, VIRGINIA BEACH, VIRGINIA 23451
(757) 422-6444

Please send _____ cookbooks   @ $19.95 _____
    Postage and handling: Total for 1 book $ 5.00 _____
                          Total for 2 to 6 books $ 9.00 _____
                                         GRAND TOTAL _____

❏ Check   ❏ Money Order

Make check or money order payable to: **Women of Galilee Cookbook**

Name _____

Address _____

City _____ State _____ Zip _____

MAIL TO: LOAVES & FISHES, Vol. 5
GALILEE GIFTS, 3928 PACIFIC AVENUE, VIRGINIA BEACH, VIRGINIA 23451
(757) 422-6444

Please send _____ cookbooks   @ $19.95 _____
    Postage and handling: Total for 1 book $ 5.00 _____
                          Total for 2 to 6 books $ 9.00 _____
                                         GRAND TOTAL _____

❏ Check   ❏ Money Order

Make check or money order payable to: **Women of Galilee Cookbook**

Name _____

Address _____

City _____ State _____ Zip _____

MAIL TO: LOAVES & FISHES, Vol. 5
GALILEE GIFTS, 3928 PACIFIC AVENUE, VIRGINIA BEACH, VIRGINIA 23451
(757) 422-6444

Please send _____ cookbooks   @ $19.95 _____
    Postage and handling: Total for 1 book $ 5.00 _____
                          Total for 2 to 6 books $ 9.00 _____
                                         GRAND TOTAL _____

❏ Check   ❏ Money Order

Make check or money order payable to: **Women of Galilee Cookbook**

Name _____

Address _____

City _____ State _____ Zip _____